MORE UNTAMED DEVOTIONS

Staci

May you meet the Untamed God of love in these pages.

Psalm 144:1

MORE UNTAMED DEVOTIONS

SHANE ALLEN BURTON

Henschel
HAUS
publishing, inc.
www.henschelHAUSbooks.com

MILWAUKEE, WISCONSIN

Published by
HenschelHAUS Publishing, Inc.
www.henschelHAUSbooks.com

ISBN: 978159598-767-9
E-ISBN: 978159595-768-6
LCCN: 2020937659

Please contact the publisher for additional information on quantity
discounts for academic and non-profit organizations.

Cover design by Lisa Kindle, www.artsoulliving.com

DEDICATION

This book is first of all dedicated to you, Dani. You are my best, good friend. You're the peas to my carrots. You are my anchor who stops me from floating off into space. You are a living reminder daily...of Grace.

Thank you for *re*-minding me...for helping me back into my right mind. You restored my shepherd's heart. You made it okay for me to Love what I Love and to enjoy what I enjoy without apology.

You didn't force me into a box. You allowed me to be me.

You are both the most Buddhist Christian I know...and the most Christian Buddhist I know. You are the Yin to my Yang.

I want to thank you for the last thousand years...and for the thousands yet to come. For my soul knew you when we met. And as much as we both fought it because of our old relationship wounds, there was enough Hope within each of us to believe in us.

And I do. And I always will.

I also dedicate this to all of my children: both the ones I've had the blessing of fathering, and those who've come into my life later. Patrick, Tucker, Darby, Zander, Cole, Lilliana, Josh, Rachel, and Isaac: I Love each of you uniquely. And my heart is filled with pride for each of you. I invite each of you into both books so that you would learn to heal from your wounds, remove your masks, and live more Freely and authentically.

Be yourselves. Don't worry about fitting into anyone else's boxes of who they perceive you to be, or who they ask you to be.

Be yourselves. Unapologetically, irrevocably, authentically you.

Please. I believe your Joy depends on it. And I believe the more Joy you experience, the greater the propensity you will have for Love.

Dani...kids...I Love you. With all of my heart. And whether this reaches you directly from me...or if I've already gone and you're getting this from these pages: I LOVE YOU.

Dani, I have been so proud to be your husband and you are my hallelujah. Kids, I have been so proud to be your daddy. You are each the greatest blessings to me.

Love,
Shane Allen Burton

TABLE OF CONTENTS

ACKNOWLEDGMENTS

I want to acknowledge some people without whom this work would never have come into being. And to start, I want to thank someone who has become a supporter, encourager, challenger, and friend, my publisher Kira Henschel. Kira, you are a gift and a blessing in this world to so many. Thank you for giving LIFE to this work and for helping me to share a message of Love with this world. Thank you as well for encouraging me to LIVEINALL-CAPS and for believing in me.

I also want to thank Lisa Kindle of Art Soul Living for her work on the cover for this book. She also did the cover for my first book, and her work here is inspired, as always. You are a gift to work with, and I'm thankful for your friendship, Lisa.

A special thank you to Rachel M. Anderson of RMA Publicity for helping this work to reach a broader audience. Thank you for pushing me and challenging me as well!

Thank you to Nicole Remini, Bill Easum, and Cindy Dingwall for reading this work and recommending it. You all have no idea what that means to me other than for me to do my best to tell you here. Nicole, you are a dear friend and someone I respect so deeply for your servant leadership in this world. Bill, you've known me for years, have allowed me to participate in some of your work, and have encouraged and challenged me in mine. You are a prophet of Light and Love. And Cindy, from my earliest days of ministry, you've been there as a boisterous, Loving presence. As you wrote so many books that instructed so many children's lives in their faith, you also encouraged me to write my own. Thank you.

A special thank you to my sister Kammi for being one of my best friends on this planet, and for believing in me and being by my side through the battle of these last couple of years. Thank you as well to all of my children and to my beautiful wife, Dani. Thank you all for putting up with me every time I've said: "I need to write."

And a HUGE thank you to all who've been so support-ive over the past two years as I've battled cancer. I can't even begin to name you all. There are literally thousands of you. And so, I hope this book reaches you all...and blesses each of you.

~ Shane Allen Burton

PREFACE

Love.

Seems pretty simple, doesn't it? But it often isn't. Maybe it's because "religion" adds and modifies and qualifies it, making it about so much that it's not? Or maybe it's our woundedness that gets in the way? All of those emotional gashes and scars from earlier in life that create unhealthy patterns of behavior and responses that cause more destruction in and around us? Or maybe it's just sometimes a hard thing to do?

I don't think there's a simple answer to this question. But the ultimate answer to it all seems to be fairly simple: Love.

When the Big Guy was asked to sum up all of what we call the Old Testament, he said: "Love the Lord, your God with all your heart, mind, soul, and strength" and "Love your neighbor as yourself.

Love God. Love people.

Simple. Right?

Basically it all comes down to Love. If it's Loving, do that. If it's not, knock it off.

And yet, it's so hard. Because what I feel like doing or saying isn't always Loving. When that jerk cuts me off in traffic, I want to speed up, honk my horn, and flip them the bird.

Yeah, that's a Loving thing to do, right? I often fail to consider that maybe the driver just got a call from their spouse saying that they're on their way to the emergency room? No, I get wrapped up in my own sense of entitlement and personal offense and...and I'll show *them*. Right?

No. Not right. Love must rule more and more in my heart.

It must. For all of us. And for that to happen, we need to heal from our hurts. We need to get intentional about the wounds of our past, heal from them as much as possible, and then decide to move on and to choose Love. And we must get past this in our faith communities as well. We sanitize our passion, tame it, and ultimately sacrifice it on the altar of religion, political correctness, and social decorum and we end up with a lack of Love. And we need to choose the more difficult path because Love is often hard. If you have children, you know this to be true.

And learning to accept Love is often a challenge, isn't it? We often view expressions of Love through our wounded lenses and thus, we are suspicious. For surely, they can't *really* Love me, right? But it's hard, because along the way, we've been hurt. And we build walls around our hearts so that no one can hurt us again. And in doing so, we build walls around our hearts that also prevent Love from getting in. And we facilitate our own self-fulfilling prophecies: we are un-Lovable.

What I propose in all of these short devotions is all about Love. And I think it starts within each one of us. We are told to Love our neighbor as ourselves. And I believe we often do. We do a terrible job of Loving our neighbors because we don't Love ourselves. We believed the lies we were told by society, by magazines, by our wounds: we are un-Lovable.

So, dear friend, hear this clearly: you are Lovable and Love-*able*. You, *just as you are*, with all of your wounds, faults, failures...and all of your healing, strengths, successes, and wonderfulness are Lovable. And you are Love-*able*...you are able to Love others. But we will do better at this when we begin to recognize those lies, and we take a stand, and we heal.

I also want to be clear about something: I don't have this down yet. I'm working on it. At times I've done a terrible job. I've hurt those around me...sometimes even intentionally. And where I've recognized this, I've done my best to seek restitution, forgiveness, and to do better at Loving. And for those times I've not recognized it, I am open to growth, learning, and awareness.

I just want to do better at Loving. I want it to overflow, and for it be a natural thing...as natural as breathing.

So as you read, know that my heart in all of this is simply that you would feel Loved, and learn to Love more. There is no condemnation here. Just Love.

And I Love you.

PROLOGUE

Before we dive in, I want to share a bit of theology—my beliefs about God. I think it's important, so as you read, you can understand more of my heart in my writing. And let me tell you this: as I've gotten older, my theology has gotten far more simple. And while I am not comparing myself to the great German theologian Karl Barth, I resonate with something he said. Later in life, he was asked to sum up his theology. And one would think that such a learned and well-written man would have some incredibly verbose and profound things to say. And yet here's how he answered the question:

"Jesus loves me, this I know. For the Bible tells me so."

I can get behind that. I can understand it. And it informs the basis of my theology quite a bit: Love God. Love people.

That being said, as you read, keep these things in mind when these terms come up:

God

It says in 1 John 4 that God is Love. And I take this quite literally. It is the foundation of my theology and so I interchangeably use these words: God and Love. Wherever you see me use the word God, try inserting the word Love. Wherever you see the word Love, insert God. Also, God is often referred to as our Heavenly Father. But the word Jesus used was abba. And the best translation we have for this word would be daddy. And what a difference. Daddy is so intimate—so familiar...even tender. Father seems so formal. I resonate more with God as daddy/mommy than the oh-so-formalized father/mother.

JESUS

I believe he was who he said he was: God. And thus, Jesus is God in the flesh. Love incarnate. Jesus is the living embodiment of Love. And that all of what he did was to Love us, and show us how to Love one another. And any God who would choose to come into the world in flesh and blood as an infant to literally become Love in the flesh, is an Untamed, very *wild* God indeed.

SIN

The stupid stuff we do out of our woundedness. Often in life, we were hurt. And those un-healed hurts tend to come out sideways in our lives and cause more hurt, either to ourselves, or others, or both. This is sin. And the more we heal, the better we learn to Love and to be Loved, and the less sin tends to happen in and around us. As we heal, we create a greater propensity to Love and to be Loved...to accept it. And in Jesus, we see the living embodiment of Love and ultimately of healing from our woundedness, and thus the path of what we often refer to as repentance, which literally means to turn away from. In Jesus, we see the path of turning away from our sin—the stupid stuff we do out of our woundedness—and turning toward a path of Love.

Love God. Love people. How hard can it be?

Untamed,
Shane Allen Burton

44

I stood in line to fill out a form with information including my name, address, the number of people living in my household, as well as my income. I was then given a number and ushered into a room filled with seating for about 200 of which, about 50 seats were taken. I was torn between gratitude and shame.

My friend, a pastor, stood in front of the room calling out numbers drawn randomly from a plastic tub. I watched the faces of those around me. Some were hopeful, their faces excited to receive gifts of food. Some were ashamed, their heads hung low, gazes downcast. There were children present assisting their parents. And there were some who were quite used to this and came prepared with their own bags and boxes with which they would use to gather gifts of sustenance to bring home to their families.

"44," said the pastor.

It only took about ten minutes before my number was called. I looked up. My eyes met hers. A half smile formed on my face...and on hers. It was awkward...probably for both of us.

I walked to the front, took the orange piece of paper from her with my number: 44. I then walked into the lobby of the church, took a box and a couple of bags, and began to receive food. Bacon, bread, yogurt, cereal, soup, vegetables, Koolaid Jammers, bottled water, lotion, sausage, breakfast sandwiches, potatoes, and...and...

And a huge, chunky, undercooked piece of humble pie.

Torn between gratitude and shame.

I know my need. I've been unemployed and my funds are woefully inadequate. Some friends have reached out to help pay my bills. And each time I've felt the same thing: torn between gratitude and shame.

What I've come to realize is this: Giving is easy. Receiving is not.

To be the one in need...to have to receive help...and sometimes ask for it is so hard. And thus I want to challenge you, friend. You are reading this from some place of comfort, I'm certain. Maybe you're on your smart phone? Or maybe you're sipping a nice rich mocha from a name brand coffee shop? From your bed? On the couch? At the desk in the den? Comfort. And as you sit there, you have the ability to give something to someone. My challenge is this: do your best to understand what it is to *receive.*

Empathize with those who must receive. So that when you give next time, do so not just with compassion for their need, but empathy for what it feels like to be torn between gratitude and shame.

Can you do that?

Because when you are in a place to give, it is a place of privilege and blessing. And it is so much easier to have the ability to give, rather than the need to receive.

Giving is easy. Receiving is not.

Thank you friends. Thanks to each of you who've reached out with words of encouragement, prayer, offers to pay bills...and for you my friends who fed me and my family today.

I am grateful. I am. I'm overwhelmed with gratitude to each of you...and for each of you. You are angels. Truly. Angel comes from the Greek word *angelos* and it means "messenger of God."

For that is what you are when you give. But remember what it is to receive and how it feels.

As I finished, a man from the church offered to help carry the groceries to my car. When we arrived and loaded them in, he offered to pray for me. I did not tell him who I was. I did not tell him I was a pastor, and that I was the one who usually prays for people. I didn't tell him I was the one who is used to giving food to those in need.

I bowed my head, and number 44 received.

REFINER OF SILVER
PSALM 66:10
ZECHARIAH 13:9

Once upon a time, God was out walking on the side of a mountain. God looked out over the land and sighed at its beauty. And contemplated things not remotely understood by God's children. God knew the nature and identity of every pebble beneath his feet...every atom of oxygen...every photon of light. Such all-encompassing awareness would be overwhelming, and yet to God, a glorious symphony.

While walking, God came upon a rough chunk of silver ore. It was lumpy, its surface cold and hard. There were lines of silver all through the hunk of ore. And yet, there were so many impurities...so many irregularities. There was so little silver that there was barely a glint in the sunlight. And yet, when God looked, God saw the glint. It was barely perceptible...but it was there.

God looked at the hunk of silver ore and knew its nature and what had to be done. And so God chose the hunk of ore from among the other rocks. He picked you up. God brought you to his smithy. He set you upon the shelf. There were preparations yet to be made.

First, he had to ready the tools. And then, God began to stoke the fire...nurturing its heat with the mighty power of his bellows, blowing energy and power into the fire until it glowed vermilion.

And there you sat, wondering...waiting. Why did God pick you up? You were content to remain among the other rocks. You were not looking to relocate...you were not looking to be chosen...and yet...

And yet...you were. Why? Why you? Why would anyone select a hunk of raw ore? What did God see in you? What plan did God have for using you? Why did you have to wait?

Waiting is hard. Especially when you don't even know for what it is you're waiting. All you knew as you sat there upon that shelf was that it was getting hotter and hotter in that room and you didn't like the looks of some of those tools. You certainly didn't like the looks of that fire. What purpose did the fire have? And why were you in the same room with it?

God sat patiently pumping, blowing his breath into the flames to make the vermilion change to argent white. When that happened, you saw God smile. Why? you wondered. What was so special about the fire being that hot? Why did it matter? God saw the argent heat, and then turned to you. He smiled reassuringly, with both Love and compassion. And somehow, you knew that meant that you were in for something...that there was some connection with you and the fire. What could it possibly be? God then selected a pot...one with a spout on one side. It was rough and worn with use...the outside of it crusty and black...the inside smooth as polished obsidian. He hung the pot over the fire.

You would later learn that the pot served a special purpose...smelting.

God rose from tending the fire. In his place, an angel sat, tenderly, steadily working the bellows. The angel was glorious and reflected the argent white of the heat...reflected the glow of Love. You blinked at the brightness of the angel and then looked back to God. He strode across the room to where you sat upon the shelf. Your waiting time seemed to be over. You became tense.

What was God doing? Why? You were apprehensive...afraid even. But then you noticed again his smile. God knew what he was doing. He'd planned it. He saw what would be...even though you did not. There was reassurance there. He lifted you off the shelf. He cradled you Lovingly in the palm of his hand. Even though you don't know what was to be, you knew that you felt peace in God's palm as his fingers enfolded you in serenity. God carried you across the room. God looked to the crucible and then back at you.

And said, "This is going to hurt."

You asked, "Why?"

He said, "Because you must be cleansed."

"Of what?" you ask.

"Of all your impurities. They are abhorrent to me. I want you to be pure. But don't worry, I won't do it all at once. You couldn't handle everything all at once. I will work little by little to purify you, dear one."

"But...I'm...scared." You said tentatively.

"I know...and that is okay. All trials are scary...all fires burn and cause pain. And pain is a very scary thing. But it's necessary."

"But why me? Why now? Why does it have to hurt?" you asked hurriedly, trying to divert God's attention from the task at hand.

"Why you? Because I chose you. Why now? Because it is time. Why does it have to hurt? Because pain and suffering cause endurance and will teach you many things." He said to you.

"Not me...not now!" you pleaded.

"But it is your time, dear one. And I will watch over you always." God said to you reassuringly.

And then God moved his gentle hand over the crucible which had begun to be heated. God gently placed you there. And it was warm...hot even. And you were scared. And you looked up to God and you saw into his eyes and you found strength waiting for you there. Maybe it would be okay...*maybe.*

The smelter was lowered closer and closer to the flames until it rested upon the white-hot coals.

You screamed.

It was a cry from the depths of your soul. Never had you felt such pain. Never had you experienced such a loss. Never had you known such an utter scraping of each and every neuro-synapse. The pain was argent white... pure... holy...like the Love who looked upon you with such great care as you writhed in pain. You wondered briefly what kind of sadistic Being would do such a thing...but then you began to sense something. A change. Deep inside the core of who you were. You were beginning to flow...to melt...to surge into a new form of being. And you saw the blatant impurities, the slag of your existence. And then you sensed them rising to the surface.

The angel pumped the bellows to keep the flame pure, sensing God's will. And then abated the pumping, knowing that Love was about to do a great work in you.

God—*Love* looked upon you and saw the slag covering the top of the crucible. God saw the more obvious impurities of your existence floating upon the surface of your new form, and asked you a question:

"Will you let go of these things for Love...and so that you might become the best version of yourself?"

The answer seemed obvious. You sensed something different within yourself now...something...better...purer. You were okay with the fact that God was asking you to let go of these things.

"Yes, for You...and for me too, I guess. Because I'm worth it, aren't I?" you answered, a new confidence arose from within you.

And then Love took an iron rod and scraped the slag of filth from the top of your new form. You sensed an immense weight and pressure lifted. You took a breath for the first time in a very long time and it came more easily.

You breathed again. Free. Yes, you felt free for the first time ever. A new Joy flooded your soul as you reveled in this change that overtook you. You knew your Joy came from Love—from God. You knew this change was the handiwork of Love at work within you. You began to understand new things about the universe. You saw new things through new eyes. You began to sense the great latticework of creation within all things and see the mark of Love throughout.

The smelting pot within which you rested was being raised. And suddenly you felt yourself traveling down a chute and being poured out into a new form. You were a New Creation. You had a new shape...a new identity and it is within Love that you found your meaning.

You sat in the mold for a time and then Love took you from the mold and thrusted your cooling form into icy water. A cry of surprise escaped your lips as you felt the finality of your new form. And like refreshing rain in the morning, you sighed with contentment. You were new. You felt complete.

And then God turned to you with something new in his eyes. You saw a look there that said this was not the end of what was in store for you.

God laid a hand on you, caressing your surface with adoration.

And then you heard Love say, "My dear one, I am refining you as silver. And yet, you are not yet ready. You are not yet pure. There are still deep-seeded impurities within you. There are still fractional amounts of slag that lurk within your shiny depths. These are not pleasing to my sight. In fact, I see a new impurity forming even as we speak...it's name is pride. You are proud of your new form and want to show it off. That is good, as long as you acknowledge the Source of the goodness...as long as you acknowledge Love. However, you are feeling proud about yourself and not Love. I must refine you further. You are almost pure...almost the best version of yourself... *almost.*"

"But," you protested, "what else is there to do? I am a New Creation in Love! I am complete! I am...I am..."

"No, *I AM*." said Love.

You hung your head in shame, realizing that you overstepped your bounds. You realized again your place within the order of all things. You the creation...not the Creator. You are not sovereign...in fact, when you tried to control your life, it seemed all too often to end up in a terrible mess...the purity of your silver tarnished beyond recognition. Love is Sovereign. Only Love reigns...only Love has control...only God knows what is best for you.

Your shame turned to submission. You laid your will out before God. You offered Love your heart. And you asked for help to remove any remaining impurities.

And Love accepted.

Again you were placed within the crucible. Again you were heated. You were melted. And little by little, the impurities embedded within you began to shake free from your grasp and rise to the surface. Again, God took the iron rod and slaked the slag from your surface.

And this time, Love looked down upon you and smiled. For there, in front of God's eyes, Love was reflected in your surface.

The smile turned into a grin. God was pleased. God saw what you became. God saw Love in you. And joy leaped within God as he saw your new form. A cry escaped God's lips and he did a little happy dance around the smithy. The angel working the bellows joined in. A holy celebration!

Again you were cooled...again thrust into the water. This time, it was complete. You were molded and shaped, heated and fired, tried and tested. You grew. You aged. You matured. You conquered. You triumphed over your impurities with Love. Through no other means would it have been possible. Without Love, you would still be that old hunk of raw ore. Rough. Irregular.

If it had not been for Love, noticing the beauty deep within you, you would still be stuck amongst the other rocks. But Love chose you. Love shaped you. Love heated you and tested you. Love refined you so much that Love is now able to be seen reflected within your surface. You chose to become the best version of yourself through Love.

And God loves you.

And you love God.

And silver is a conductor...a conductor of Love...a conduit of adoration which spills out to those around you...to all of the other rocks, waiting to have their beauty brought forth from their depths...so they too, will reflect the face of Love.

You have been refined...and now you are the finest silver, reflecting God to a world that needs to see.

EDELWEISS, DANCING, AND SMILES

"Ms. Perkins, you have stage 4, small-cell adenocarcinoma and it is terminal." This was the death sentence pronounced by the oncologist to my fifty-year-old mother in October of 2001.

My mother turned to me looking like a scared six-year old child, bewildered by the words from the doctor. "What's that mean? Shane, what does that mean?"

I turned to my mom. I knew what the oncologist meant. And now I was acting as translator and son simultaneously as I grasped my mother's hands tightly in my own, trying as translator to tell my mom she was going to die, and as son, to do so as gently as possible.

"Mom," I paused, feeling my throat rapidly wanting to swell shut to choke back the words I didn't want to believe, let alone say, "It means that you have lung cancer and you're going to die."

And there it was.

My mom was dying.

Seven short weeks later, on December 14th, 2001, my sister Kammi and I held our mother, all sixty-five pounds of her, in our arms. Her breathing struggled to gain purchase. After each exhalation, we waited wondering if it would be her last. As we sat there rocking her and holding her, our cousins Tami and Shawn showed up to join us in the dimly lit room at Guardian Angel's in Elk River, Minnesota.

A couple of hours earlier, I had gotten the phone call from the hospice nurse telling me to come as soon as possible as she believed my mom was in the last hours of her life. I drove with an intensity to get there before she passed, and equal amounts of not wanting to face the reason I was driving in the first place.

As I drove I reminisced about my mom. She was a woman who, in spite of a rough childhood, grew up knowing how to celebrate life. The reason I love to dance so much is because of her. She danced everywhere: out with friends listening to bands on the weekends, outside on our patio listening to music, in the morning in the kitchen making us breakfast, in the evening in the kitchen making us dinner, around the house as she cleaned. She danced. And when she danced, she smiled. She truly came alive. It was a gift to see.

She was a gift. And each day, to her, was as well.

She loved the music and dancing in her favorite movie, *The Sound Of Music.* Her favorite song? *Edelweiss.*

She would ask me to play it on the piano for her any time we came across one.

And thus, in the moments leading to her last, while cradling her in my arms as she once did me, I began to sing.

> *"Edelweiss, edelweiss,*
>> *Every morning you greet me.*
> *Soft and white, clean and bright,*
>> *You look happy to meet me.*
> *Blossom of snow may you bloom and grow,*
>> *Bloom and grow forever.*
> *Edelweiss, edelweiss, bless my*
>> *Homeland forever."*

And as I sang the last lines regarding blessings of my homeland, my beautiful mother, Paulette Marie Perkins, breathed her last. One final exhalation, and my sister, cousins, and I sobbed.

That was nineteen years ago.

Recently, I was walking through my place of employment and I ran into a fellow employee named Cathy who was a cashier. I didn't know exactly how old she was, but I knew she was older than me.

And I knew her smile. It was pure radiance...the purest Joy.

And what was tremendous to me about this, is Cathy had been battling cancer for a while. I didn't know what kind or what stage. But I knew she'd gone through radiation and chemotherapy treatments a few times. She continued as a cashier for a long time after she lost all her hair. It didn't seem to get her down. She still smiled. She still brought her Joy with her every single day. And the retail environment in which we worked—well, let's just say it wasn't exactly all puppy-dogs and kittens, sunshine and lollipops.

But Cathy smiled like it was.

When I saw her, she was shopping as a customer. As soon as our eyes met, she hit me with it. My heart was lighter. My spirit began to overflow with the same Joy she carried. My face couldn't resist. I smiled...*no*, I grinned when I saw her. I felt younger. I felt child-like. She greeted me and asked how I was doing. I responded, "Cathy, I have no complaints."

I went on to say how much of an inspiration she was to me. I told her that when I saw her, anything about which I had to complain faded completely and was replaced by a smile. And then I asked her, "Cathy, how is it that in spite of having cancer, going through all your treatments, losing your hair, and everything else...how is it that you smile?"

As I told her how she's an inspiration to me, her smile grew larger, and she began to cry tears of Joy.

I confess, I began to sob with her, right in the main aisle of our store with customers and other employees all around me.

Cathy responded with an even larger smile saying, "I have to! Each day is a gift."

Each day is a gift. And Cathy was another gift in my day. Such a wondrous gift, I had to share it. Because gifts are meant to be shared.

I called my friend J.M. to tell her of this inspirational woman named Cathy and she got excited and told me of her friend who found out she had cancer.

They had coffee together. They had their normal small talk. And then the conversation shifted. J.M.'s friend got a bit serious and told her, "I have cancer."

My friend J.M. began to cry at the news.

And her friend, her body riddled with cancer, leaned closer, smiled and said, "J.M., it is not the time for crying. Now is the time for smiling and *living*."

And I can't help but smile once again as I write this. I hope you are too. If you're not, find something that will make you smile. Go hug your child, or a friend. Look up a joke. Eat some ice cream. Stomp in a puddle. Make a snow angel. Make a fart sound with your hand in your armpit. I don't care what it is, but for goodness' sake, find something to make you smile.

Because each day is a gift.

So smile. Dance. And whatever that thing is that you've been putting off...maybe you should do it?

Call that person. Hug someone. Forgive. Laugh. Smile. Go on a trip. Get lost. Eat ice cream for breakfast with your children. Dream your dreams and then LIVE them. Give to those in need. Never pass up a lemonade stand, or a hug from a kid, or a chance to get dirty and play. Those things you've half-jokingly talked about doing as your "Bucket List?" Do them. Now.

We are given three hundred and sixty-five gifts each year to open with Joyful expectancy.

Open your gifts. Because now is the time for LIVING, for smiling, and for dancing.

AN EAGLE'S PROMISES

Inspired by my server on my cruise-ship, Ayu, who works tirelessly for her family with an exuberance for loving and serving her guests...all because she wants to provide for her family...especially her little girl, Lica, back in Bali, Indonesia.

PSALM 91

Once upon a time, there was a Mother Eagle, maternal, yet fierce, magnificent in her beauty, and frightening in her intensity. Through her fierce determination, she had constructed her aerie, weaving together sticks, branches, and other things to provide protection for what would soon arrive. As the days passed, she fed herself well, building up precious layers of nourishment within her body, for the clutch that would form within her.

And then it happened. She only laid one egg in this clutch. Daily, she sat upon it, providing it warmth, Love, and protection. She spoke to her egg daily saying, "Little One, right now you can't see me, but I am here. You can't feel me, but you feel the warmth of my body. And while you don't hear my words, you do hear my voice and I know one day, you will recognize it."

Weeks passed by and the embryo inside that egg grew into a young eaglet. No longer could the egg contain it's prize. The egg began to rock back and forth and Mother Eagle began to speak encouragingly to her offspring. The words were muffled to the eaglet's ears, but the tone was unmistakable. There was Love there.

The eaglet began to peck away at her incubator and soon a beam of light shone through. And the words of encouragement became clear: "You can do it, my Love! I am here. Even though you can't see me, you soon will. Even though you can't feel me, soon you will find shelter in the shadow of my wings. Even though you couldn't hear me, now you can, and you know my voice."

And through the struggle, the young eagle freed herself from the confines of the shell, being pulled swiftly into the care of her mother. With scrutiny, Mother Eagle inspected her baby, ensuring health. Always speaking words of Love and encouragement, Mother Eagle cleaned her eaglet of the remains of her life before inside the egg.

After a while, the young eaglet began to feel a new sensation in her belly. She asked her mother what the growly feeling was.

"That is called hunger, young one. And that means I must get you food...something to eat."

And with that, Mother Eagle hunched down, gathering power in her legs and mighty wings, and then launched herself into flight. The young eaglet looked in wonder upon the majesty of Mother Eagle, and for a moment forgot about everything around her. But it slowly began to dawn upon her, that Mother Eagle was flying away, becoming smaller and smaller. A new feeling welled up within the young eaglet. She felt frantic, alone...she felt...*fear*. And after a while, she could endure this feeling no longer and began to cry out for Mother Eagle.

"Mother! Mother, where did you go? Why did you leave me?" Young Eaglet cried out many more times, and then in the distance, she saw a speck. And from a distance, she could hear a Voice calling back to her. Eventually that speck turned into Mother Eagle, and words became clear.

"I am coming, my Love. I was never far."

Mother Eagle had returned with food for Young Eaglet, and the fear of just a minute ago was replaced once again with pangs of hunger. Mother Eagle fed her child and once the food was gone, Young Eaglet, filled with words, could no longer contain herself.

"Mother, where did you go? Why did you leave? I was so afraid? How could you do something like that? I am so little and I felt so alone."

Mother Eagle smiled and gathered her words. She looked adoringly upon Young Eaglet and in her rich, maternal voice began to speak: "My Heart, there are times you can't see me. But I am never far away. I will never leave you or forsake you, dear one. Though I may be miles away, I am always close enough to be there when needed.

My Love, there are times you can't feel me, but you can feel the nest I've created for you. You can feel the protection I've provided for you. You can feel your full belly and know that I've fed you.

And my Dear One, there are times you can't hear me. But you remember the sound of my voice. And even though you can't hear me, I hear you. If you call, I will answer.

For you see, Beloved, you are mine. And I Love you."

As she said these last words, she placed her wing over Young Eaglet, sheltering her, becoming a living refuge...her Mother.

THE GREAT SQUIRREL RAID

PHILIPPIANS 2: 14-16

I sat at my computer, checking my email, when I heard the beginning of a noise which would come to haunt me. *Scritch. Scritch—scriiiittch—scri-scri-scriiiitttccchhh.*

I stopped typing. I looked around. For the life of me, I couldn't see from whence the horrifying sound had originated. I tried to shake off the effects of the noise and go back to responding to the email sent to me. Valiantly did I try. But alas, it was to no avail. For as I sat there, the terror of that noise began to scratch away at my sanity.

Scritch. Scritch—scriiiittch—scri-scri-scriiiitttccchhh.

I stopped typing again. I looked around, yet again. I cocked my head to the side, listening for the origin of the evil sound I was hearing. I still couldn't pinpoint the location. It sounded like it was coming from across the room. But that was impossible. I was home alone. At the time, we didn't have pets. And I was still fairly certain of my sanity. With a deep breath, and a far-from-effortless attempt at resuming my work, I put all of what remained of my resolve into typing.

Scritch. Scritch—scriiiittch—scri-scri-scriiiitttccchhh.

My head snapped up. Finally, I could sense the exact direction from which the sound had come. It came from the sliding glass doors in our family room. At first, I thought maybe a friend was playing a joke. But the sound did not come from such a height as to warrant human origin. I looked lower. And there it was. A squirrel, scritching away furiously, trying to find a way into my abode. I laughed out loud at the sight.

Resuming my work yet again, I dove back into typing my email responses to my friends. Within a few minutes, there was another squirrel at the sliding glass doors. And he or she (I'm not the Resident Squirrel Expert) began the furious scritching, trying to get into our domain. And yet again, I laughed and resumed working.

Not five minutes later, a third squirrel joined the attempt! I'm not remotely kidding. Squirrels had descended upon my residence and there was something they desperately wanted from within my house. The squirrels had organized. I imagined some hideout in the hollow tree in our yard with charts of possible points of entry stuck to the walls of their hideout. They had done their reconnaissance. They knew their escape routes should they find themselves under enemy surveillance. But when they eventually got to the sliding glass doors, exhausting all other entry attempts, all of their planning went out the window. They were desperate. They were going nuts trying to get in.

Because there was something inside that they wanted.

So would so many people out there, if only we would live our lives of faith as if it made a difference. If we actually lived lives of Love, there would be something inside they wanted as well.

If we lived in such a way, that it was obvious to people that Love was in our lives and that it actually made the difference Jesus claimed it would when he was on earth with the disciples, then people would be clamoring...scritching away...trying to find a way into such a Life. So often, we live dutiful lives of faith, filled with resignation to our fates, and a look of determination on our faces. We live with such an utter lack of Joy and exuberance, that it's no wonder the world looks at us and doesn't get it. If they saw instead, the great celebration that is a Life of Love, then we wouldn't be able to keep up with the converts. You think I'm kidding?

When you read in the book of Acts, that literally thousands of people were joining in with Peter and the disciples, it's not because they were walking around dour-faced and sullen. People were joining in because of the extreme difference they saw Love making in the lives of those first century men and women.

I heard once that a grumpy-looking Christian man was asked if he was joyful. And his response was "Yes, of course I am!" To which the questioner said, "Well then, tell your face!"

My friends, tell your face that you're joyful! Tell your face that Love is in your heart! Remind your face of the Joy you first felt when you realized the difference Love was making in you. We're supposed to be a "breath of fresh air," says Paul in his letter to the church at Philippi. We're supposed to show people a glimpse of good living and of the Living God...of LOVE.

Hello! Smile, gosh-darn it! Sing a song. Skip for crying out loud! I don't care if you're wearing dress shoes...you remember how, don't you? Now get up, bring a cup of coffee to a co-worker with a smile on your face. Send flowers to your spouse for no reason. Surprise somebody with Joy today. Tell someone they're awesome...and mean it. Give a hug...a high-five...or even five dollars. Live the difference Love is making in your life!

And when someone asks you, "Hey! What's up with you?" Tell them. Tell them that it's because you want to Live a life of Love. And let them chew on that for a while. Let them mull it over. Let them stew even. Because they're going to see this difference...they're going to know the

Source of this difference...and then they're going to desire it.

Pretty soon, you'll find them scritching away, trying to get in. And you'll be there, ready and waiting, to welcome them into this good life of Love. People are going to go nuts tryin' to get in on this life of faith, if only we would live in such a way to show the difference Love makes in our lives. People would stand in line waiting to get into worship, goin' nuts to get in. Imagine standing-room-only in our worship services! Can you? I can...and it makes me even more joyful to think about it.

Live the difference, my friends. And people are going to go nuts trying to get in on it.

Right In Front Of Your Face

Psalm 73: 1-5

A couple of years ago, after a particularly heavy snowfall, I had to go out to excavate our driveway from the mountain of crystallized water that had formed there. I was not excited about the prospect of such a task. So, I did what any self-respecting Minnesotan without a working snowblower would do: I hired the neighbor kid to come over and blow out our driveway for $25 (I know, it's a lot...but the bottom of the driveway was about three and a half feet deep because of the plow going by).

Realizing that we could not continue to keep paying these amounts of cash to the teenaged extortionist who lived across the street ("Give me the money or you'll never leave your house again," followed by maniacal laughter, reminiscent of an old Vincent Price film), I decided upon the next snowfall, I would go out to the shed, and try to resurrect our snowblower. I went out there armed with wrenches, screwdrivers, warm clothes, and a can of noxious multipurpose starting/cleaning fluid which is also good for removing nail polish, tar, and head-lice. I pulled out the spark plug, put in a new one, checked the gap, poured some of the explosive fluid into the chamber, cleaned the spark-plug cable connection and put everything back together.

I then steeled myself for pulling the starting cable. I braced my feet. I put my left hand down on the machine to hold it in place. And I began to pull. *Brum...* *...brum...brum.* Nothing. I pulled again. *Brum...brum...*

brum...brum. Still nothing. I pulled again and again and again. And still nothing. I adjusted the choke. I pulled several more times. I checked the gas tank. Yup. There's gas in there. I resumed pulling. In a wild frenzy, I began to pull. I pulled so fast and so hard that I actually just about fell out of the shed into the snow.

Finally, I resigned myself to the fact that the snow-blower had gone on strike and was not willing to work for me any longer. "Heck, no, I won't blow!" I turned my head to see the shovel staring at me. My shovel was just itching to be used. It was sick of life in the shed. I think maybe the snowblower and the shovel had some sort of a deal worked out. I grabbed the shovel, closed up the shed, and began to shovel the driveway.

After finishing, I went into the house, and promptly collapsed. Later in the day, I needed to go to the store for a few items. I went to leave and I couldn't find my keys. I checked my pockets. I checked all the countertops. I looked up and down to find my keys. Finally, I admitted my problem to my wife: "Have you seen my keys?"

"No," she said. "But I'll bet you lost them in the snow when you were out shoveling or trying to fix the snow-blower."

"Yeah, right!" I said, firmly denying such an absurd possibility. Why, that could never happen, could it? I couldn't be so stupid as to leave my keys in my pocket while going out to shovel, could I? Nahhh...

So, knowing that I would find the keys somewhere, I began to search again. I checked all of my pockets again. I went out to look in the car, thinking maybe I had locked them in there. I looked in the dirty clothes baskets. I checked the kids' toy box. I even cleaned off the top of my desk to look there!

No keys.

I was looking everywhere but where I needed to be looking.

Do you ever do that? Look everywhere but where you need to be looking? How often do we search for answers in the wrong places? How often do we try to fulfill our needs with everything but the right thing? Whenever I see the Powerball amount go up to an obscene number, which I could win if only I purchased the winning ticket, I see answers to my questions...millions of them. I turn on the TV and I see the Ted Turners and Bill Gates of this world with amounts of money that I can't even begin to count, much less spend, and I desire to have what they have. Wouldn't it be nice if I no longer had to worry? Wouldn't it be nice if the bill collectors forgot my phone number? Wouldn't it be great to be debt-free? Wouldn't it be nice to be able to put aside enough money to pay for all of my kids' college? Wouldn't it be nice to have that luxury car, lake home, and a new wardrobe? Wouldn't it?

Yeah, sometimes I think it would be. It would be nice. Nice and comfortable. Somehow, I don't think that's the goal for our lives. Jesus never promised comfort and niceties. In fact, quite the opposite. Jesus told the disciples to go out with nothing but the clothes on their backs and the sandals on their feet. *Luke 10:4* How's that for comfort? Jesus didn't promise that life would be nice. In fact, he said that he didn't come to bring niceness, but he came to bring a sword which would divide people. *Matthew 10:34-36*

When our lives become nice and comfortable, we become complacent. We lose any aspect of readiness that we might have once had. And Jesus warns us to be ready in Luke 10:3 "On your way! But be careful—this is hazardous work. You're like lambs in a wolf pack." Complacency, birthed out of comfort and nice-ness, causes us to look where we should not be looking. It causes us to lose our focus. It causes us to look away from what we should be seeing.

Complacency, birthed out of our lust and envy, causes us to miss seeing the goodness of Love. God is the giver of all good things. And whenever we look away from a life of Love and look to our own comfort, thinking we're looking at the real good things of life, we in fact miss the true good things of life: Love, Beauty, Joy, and Peace. When you're desiring a luxury car, you're probably forgetting the needs of the person sitting next to you. When you're envying someone for their luxury yachts and mansions, you're probably not remembering any third-world children who are thankful for a bowl of rice when they can get it.

So often, I miss seeing the goodness of God, because I'm not lookin' where I should be.

I miss Love while looking with lust and envy.

I finally admitted the folly of my ways and went out to look through the snow by the shed. First, still thinking that my keys might not be in the snow, I looked on the shelves in the shed. But then, I got really honest with myself...and with God. I prayed, thanking God for the many blessings of my life, and I asked for help in finding my keys. I reached into the snow, and after only a couple of swipes and grabs, I found them, buried about six inches deep in the snow. They had been propelled out of my pocket in the frenzy of snowblower-starting-rope-pulling madness. There they were. I looked where I was supposed to look...and there was goodness...right in front of my face.

CREAM-STYLE COUCH SUPPORT

PSALM 65:2-3

To say that my mom's family was poor would be an understatement. And to say that my grandfather was a mentally stable individual would be like ordering a cheeseburger—hold the cheese. My mom's household was a bit on the chaotic side. I'm thinking this too qualifies as an understatement. However, even in the midst of the madness, there was Love and even some modicum of responsibility.

Living from hand to mouth, their family often had to live life "as is." They accepted each other "as is." They accepted their house "as is." They never questioned where the food came from, nor what it really was...even if another pet guinea pig or rabbit was missing from the cage. They accepted it "as is." No questions asked. And when something broke, they either ignored it, tossed it, or fixed it with whatever was on hand.

As most families did, they owned a couch. Of course, the couch came to them "as is." And at some point in the tattered sofa's existence, some of its legs were broken. Now, you can't really ignore broken legs on a couch, otherwise your view of the television will be a little askew. And they couldn't really afford to buy a new couch, so tossing the old one was out of the question. And thus, my grandfather fixed the couch with whatever was on hand. Apparently, books wouldn't do the trick. I don't know; maybe they didn't have many, and the ones they had were often in use. Nor could my grandfather find something from the garage to use to replace the missing legs. After searching through the garage and the house, my grandfather at some point made it to the kitchen. And opening up one of the cupboards, an angel's light shone down upon them: some cans of cream-style corn. Mmmm...you can't help but conjure forth an image of that chunky yellow corn mixture. The 40-watt lightbulb over my grandfather's head flickered on for a brief moment. An idea had come to him: why not use cans of cream-style corn to replace the broken legs of the couch? They're just slightly larger than the original legs, plus, they're cylindrical, just like the legs were.

Scarily enough, it almost seems logical. *Almost.*

My mom's family had six children. And if you know anything about children and couches, you know that couches are meant to be jumped on, dived into, and trampled upon. An interesting thing happens when you combine the forces of speed, mass, and gravity. What weighs fifty or sixty pounds at a stand still can turn into two, three, or more times that amount of weight. A little kid, to an unsuspecting couch, can suddenly weigh in at two or three hundred pounds.

Solid, wooden legs are meant to handle such pressure. However, hollow tin cans, filled with cream-style corn are not. Eventually, one of the cans would not be able to withstand the pressure and would explode, spewing forth the chunky yellow corn substance.

Now, don't you fret...because my grandfather certainly did not. All one needed to do was wipe up the cream-style corn, and replace the exploded can with a fresh one. A fleeting fix, yielding temporary results. And so the cycle would continue. Can explodes, couch tilts, clean up the mess, and get a new can. Over and over and over again. I wonder what the local grocer thought about all the cream-style corn he sold to my mom's family?

How often do we do the same thing? How often are our fixes fleeting? How often do our attempts at taking care of something once and for all turn into transitory tries, spewing forth the chunky yellow sin substance of our lives?

And sin is really just a way for our woundedness to come out sideways. For don't we sin out of our woundedness trying to feel better for just a while? And once committed, we then have to figure out how to handle it our choices and their effects.

We endeavor in vain to cover up the effects of sin in our lives, without ever fixing the real problem. We deny our sins. We hide them. We prop up our lives with temporary legs of support which inevitably fail under the strain of the weight of our sins.

A temporary fix ain't gonna cut it.

For millennia, humankind has temporarily taken care of sin by offering up token offerings to assuage our guilt. We pretend that our minor offenses never happened, and rationalize our major ones.

We provide fleeting fixes, yielding temporary results.

But not God. God doesn't like to sweep things under the proverbial rug of our lives. Because inevitably, the rug wears out and must be replaced, or worse yet, is accidentally pulled back to reveal the chunky yellow sin substance we've hidden there. God's not into fleeting fixes.

No, God likes fixes of finality, yielding eternal results.

God, out of extravagant Love, offered his son Jesus, once and for all as THE one and only fix which would act with finality. And when we get really honest with ourselves and admit that we've screwed up, and we let God know that yes, we've screwed up...and BIG TIME...and we say we're sorry, asking for God's forgiveness, we receive the fix of finality. No can's of cream-style corn temporarily supporting our lives...but Jesus—Love incarnate—bearing the burden of our sins, and obliterating them entirely from existence, as if they'd never occurred.

I love how the songwriter, King David, says it in today's text: *"We all arrive at your doorstep sooner or later, loaded with guilt, our sins too much for us—but you get rid of them once and for all."*

Did you hear that? Once and for all! That's permanence, my friends. A done deal. Fixed forever. When we get honest with ourselves and with God about our sins, and ask for forgiveness, receiving the gift of Love and Grace, our sins are gone for good. The problem is fixed forever. God accepts you "as is." Just say it: "God, I've screwed up. You know what I've done. And I'm tired of trying to fix the problem with my measly attempts at a solution. I'm sick of cleaning up the mess, again and again. Help me God. I'm so sorry. I know I don't deserve it...how could I after the things I've done? But I'd really like to receive the gift you offer in your Son Jesus."

And that's it. A done deal. Fixed forever. At least what you've done so far. But have you addressed your woundedness? Have you sought to do what it takes to heal? Have you read the books, or gone to therapy, or journaled...or forgiven those who've hurt you? Have you truly healed from your wounds? Because if not, you're more than likely going to continue in a cycle of sin.

God takes care of the things we've already done. And God can help with our healing as well. But *we* have to get real and honest with ourselves, or our attempts at fixing will be fleeting and futile. We can continue to live in the ridiculous cycle of propping up our lives with temporary solutions which will inevitably give way to the weight of our sins. Or, we can get honest and say that we're tired of the cycle and ask for God's help to break it.

What's it gonna be? Aren't you tired of cleaning up chunky yellow sin substance? Aren't you tired of the mess it's making in your life? Yeah, me too. I'm going to cancel my standing order at the grocery store for cream-style corn and receive the gift of a permanent fix...once and for all. I'm going to do the hard work of healing...as well as ask for God's grace.

By the way, I still can't help but laugh whenever we eat cream-style corn.

30 Silver Pieces for Your Thoughts

Matthew 27:1-10

The legacy of Judas is Aceldama. Scripture calls it the Potter's Field...the place where useless broken shards were discarded...a place where pilgrims far from home were buried. But the people of the time called it by it's true name...Aceldama...

The Field of Blood.

One field...thirty silver pieces...countless graves...the price of the betrayal of the Savior.

At least we know this: both Judas, and the chief priests and elders felt some measure of guilt. Judas hung himself. And the chief priests and elders wouldn't return the silver to the temple treasury. It could not be a part of the tithe...the first fruits of labor given to the work of God. Why? Wouldn't thirty silver pieces accomplish a lot of ministry? Couldn't thirty silver pieces save some lives?

They did. For thirty pieces of silver, the Savior was betrayed...and it was through those thirty pieces that he became the Savior. For if there was no betrayal...there wouldn't have been a crucifixion. And we...you and me sitting here reading this document...we would not be washed clean. Our sins would still be a smudge upon our eternities.

They, the chief priests and elders, called it "blood money." And that's what it was...Blood of the Lamb Money.

Little did they know what they were buying when they handed those thirty paltry pieces of silver to Judas

---

Iscariot. Would they still have paid the price if they knew what it was they were purchasing? For that day...when they handed those pieces of silver to Jesus' friend...they bought Salvation for all of humankind for all of time.

Salvation was purchased that day for thirty pieces of silver. Does that thought strike you as odd? It does me. For so long, I have scoffed at Judas for accepting such a trivial sum for such a treacherous service. And now I wonder if he knew what he was buying that day. Did he have an inkling of what would be? Did he, of all the disciples, get it?

I'd like to think so. I'd like to think that Judas knew what had to be done and he did it. And being the spend-thrift he was, he haggled with the chief priests and instead of fifteen pieces of silver, he talked them into thirty. Think of the people Jesus could feed with that money! Think of how far they could carry Jesus' Message! Just think! And besides, didn't Jesus need to tone things down a bit anyway? I mean really, he was sure stepping on a lot of toes. And shouldn't he just mind his own business? It's one thing to do some healings here and there...but to meddle about in the financial affairs of wealthy young rulers and all those hawking their wares in the temple courts...I mean really!

His mind was made up. Thirty pieces of silver! He'd get them to shut Jesus up and tone things down a bit, plus, their ministry would be furthered.

It all sounds so rational, doesn't it? That's how the evil works. It takes a seemingly good idea and twists it...just...so...until it's slightly off kilter. Most won't recognize the subtle shift. But those with discerning eyes can see.

"For just one lousy kiss, I get us thirty pieces of silver, plus, I get us our lives back!" The betrayal of Jesus for thirty pieces of silver...the murder of the Savior for money...the execution of Emmanuel...God with us, but only until he's nailed on a cross...

There is yet another paradox here. The price was both too expensive and too cheap...all at the same time.

Thirty pieces of silver was both too much to pay for such a despicable deed and too little to receive to make available the most precious gift ever: Eternal Salvation.

As the cold coins caressed Judas' palms, their weight in his hands was far less than that which he carried in his soul at that moment. And with an angry rush, he scooped them up, put them in the little bag, and headed back to the temple.

He was angry. At himself. At the chief priests and the elders of the temple. And even Jesus. Why did he always have to push things so far? Why did he always speak out against the wealthy and the religious?

With tears of anger and remorse streaming down his face, Judas headed to the temple and hurled the blood money back at the priests and elders where it scattered and clinked on the temple floor, echoing the sounds Jesus made there when he overturned the tables that one day. And as grief wracked his body, guilt rocked his soul. He went to a place away from town, hung himself, where eventually, the rope gave way and his lifeless body fell, scattering his entrails on the ground. Still more blood.

He left the chief priests and elders just standing there...some with mouths agape. Others just stood there, heads hung in shame. And one by one, they began to gather silver pieces from the floor of that place of worship.

One...why did we do it?
Two...why did he do it?
Three...what were we thinking?

Four...But were we wrong? I mean, he was a menace.

Five...Yeah, but he also healed the sick, cured the lame, and helped the blind to see. Not even a sorcerer can do that.

Six...I wonder where Judas went?

Seven...I wonder what they'll do to Jesus?

Eight...I am so ashamed.

Nine...I can't tell my children...they went to him that one day.

Ten...Maybe I'll go and try to find Judas.

Eleven...I wish Judas would never come back...then no one would have to know.

Twelve...Don't go, Judas!

Thirteen...good riddance, Judas.

Fourteen...I sure pity Judas.

Fifteen...We were hoping it would only cost us this much.

Sixteen...I'll have to crawl on my hands and knees to get some of these. Huh...life sure looks different when you're on your knees.

Seventeen...Some nerve he has to give the money back!

Eighteen...My God, what have we done?!

Nineteen...I hope this doesn't get back to my family.

Twenty...Did you see how sad Judas looked?

Twenty-one...Did you see how sad Jesus looked?

Twenty-two...I wonder how I look right now?

Twenty-three...I hope they nail that Jesus guy. I've had just about all I can take from him.

Twenty-four...Why didn't he take the money and run?

Twenty-five...What are we going to do with all that money?

Twenty-six...Forgive me Father, for I knew not what I did.

Twenty-seven...Forget this, I've got better things to do than pick up a few lousy coins.

Twenty-eight: Do you think my sins could be forgiven?

Twenty-nine: Do you think that I could be healed?

Thirty:...Do you think I can be saved?

Yes, friend...of course you can be saved. Just call out to God today. Ask Love into your heart...into your life...Ask God to clean out your spiritual closet with you.

For only thirty pieces of silver, Salvation was inadvertently purchased that day. For you...for me...for Judas.

How about you, friend? Will you accept the gift? Will you not just appreciate its wrapping, but also open it up so you can receive God's greatest gift? His son...his Grace...his Love.

In case you missed it, that's us there in the temple, squatting down to pick up some silver pieces.

What are your thirty thoughts? Why don't you go make change for a dollar right now...get thirty coins. Set them in front of you...and pick them up, one-by-one. Think of that day. Think of the time in which they live. What thoughts come to your mind?

Our Savior went willingly and knowingly to the cross... knowing the price that he would pay...and that was paid.

Was it worth it?

What do you think?

A penny for your thoughts...

BABY SHOE REMINDERS

MATTHEW 19: 16-22

When's the last time you've seen your baby shoes? If you have them, dig 'em out. Put them up against your feet and see how tiny you really were! What were your thoughts at that point in your existence? What was important to you? What was most valuable to you?

My baby shoes are among the things I consider to be my most valuable possessions. I remember so many of my most valuable possessions: my stuffed Tony the Tiger and Dapper Dan, my Hong Kong Phooey lunch box, my orange banana-seat "Clean Machine" bike, a Boy Scout survival knife, two banners from different bands I was in, my stamp collection, my songs that I've written, my drawings, cartoons, and paintings, and my leather-bound, collector's copies of *The Hobbit* and *The Lord of the Rings* by J.R.R. Tolkien. Some of these are still my most prized possessions. I've added a few: my miniature version of the Mystery Machine from Scooby Doo, a spork (long story...ask me sometime in person), and my baby shoes, which my mom just gave back to me a few years ago.

My Hong Kong Phooey lunch box eventually became worn with use and we threw it away. I outgrew my Clean Machine. Tony the Tiger went the way of the trash after many years of sitting in a closet. And Dapper Dan was left behind at the doctor's office when I was about 4 years old. We went back for it, alas and forsooth, it was nowhere to be found. I still have my Boy Scout Knife, the band banners, my songs and artwork, the Tolkien books, my Mystery Machine, Spork, and my baby shoes.

In all honesty, I'd rather not get rid of any of these possessions. In so many ways, they define me. They define who I am, who I was, and from where I've come. They tell stories. They are part of my story. And yet, even if, like Dapper Dan and Tony the Tiger, these things are left behind, my story still continues. I am still me. I am no less me without these things. But I still like holding on to them as reminders. Especially these cute little baby shoes. I can't believe my feet used to be this size. And yet, here they are, physical proof of this part of my life. These now jaded feet used to kick and wiggle about in these little shoes. Imagine. These shoes are a reminder of the steps I took so long ago down the path that is my life. And all of these other things: stamps, books, songs, toys—continue to tell the story detailing other steps I've taken along my way.

There are other things I have, not possessions, but they're a part of me in so many ways: my wife, my children, my friends, and my church. And I'd rather not give up any of these things either. They're important to me. Again, they are a part of the story that is me. Talk to my wife, and you learn pieces of my story. Watch my children at play, and see the echoes of my own childhood.

In the passage of Scripture from the story of Jesus' life as told by Matthew the Tax Collector, we see an extraordinarily wealthy young man, coming to find out how to obtain the precious commodity of eternal life. I imagine this man, like everything else in his life, figured eternal life was something to be acquired as he was so used to doing. He sees Jesus talking to a crowd. He's heard the rumors: "He offers eternal life." And so our rich young man figures that Jesus is the broker with whom he needs to deal to work out the acquisition. In words which sound an awful lot like "How much is it for eternal life?" the rich young man asks what it will cost him. He's thinking in monetary terms. He's thinking that a certain dollar amount can be reached and he will simply have to produce the funds, and the deal will be done. However, he's not prepared for the price Jesus quotes him.

"Hey, fella, you want eternal life? Okay, I believe I can acquire some for you. But it's going to cost you!" says Jesus.

"Okay, how much?" asks the rich young man.

"Every last penny in your possession." says Jesus.

Imagine the reaction. Imagine how you'd feel. Because I know the things which are most precious to me. And I know the heartache I would feel to have to give them all up. Because isn't that what Jesus is really asking him? "What's most precious to you?"

The young man replies that his wealth is most precious to him.

So Jesus says, "Give it all away. Every bit of it."

The man thinks Jesus is crazy. He stands there with his mouth hanging open, saying "Jesus, you're nuts!" But he's blinded by his own insecurity. He finds security and control in his wealth. And he has no clue that security and control found in anything other than Jesus is but an illusion. So our young wealthy man, trudges off to muddle with his own thoughts. I like to think that he wrestled with this long and hard. I like to think that at some point, he realized the wisdom of what Jesus was saying and came back to follow him. But you know, Jesus didn't think he would. He said it'd be easier for someone to ride a camel through the eye of a needle than for our young wealthy man to come by eternal life. Ouch!

As a child, it was so much easier to let go of things precious to me. When I was about five or six years old, I looked at the things I held to be most dear to me and decided that I would give my most valuable item to Jesus for a birthday present. It was my Tonka toy car. I put it in the mail box with a little Happy Birthday note. It was simpler then. Life seemed a lot more clear to me. Less variables. Less information. Less complication. If Jesus told me as a child, that I'd get to hang out with him forever if only I'd give up my Dapper Dan or my Tonka car then heck, I would have given 'em up in heartbeat.

But now, it's not so easy. Now, I weigh my choices. I do cost/benefit analyses on such decisions. I think about things and discuss them. I weigh in all of the variables. I obtain more information. I do a careful web-search and look at the latest issue of *Consumer Reports* to find out more so I can make an informed decision. And in the end, I'm still left with the same insecurities and control issues our hero, the rich young man was left to wrestle with.

Just before our story of the rich young man, we see Jesus talking with some kids who busted through his armed guard to talk with their Friend. Jesus tells everyone there that they must become like these very children to enter Heaven. And so I sit here, looking at my baby-shoe-reminders of yesteryear and a light shines forth from the darkness and I nod my head knowingly. Children tend to see things a lot more clearly, I think. To them, the choice of giving up your money to be with Jesus is a huge "Duh!" They know the fun they're going to have with him. And they know his games are far better than the ones their money will buy.

It says in Matthew 5:3 "You're blessed when you've lost what's most dear to you. Only then can you be embraced by the One most dear to you."

Jesus knew that for the wealthy young man to follow him, he'd need to give up that which was most dear to him. For most of us, we'll never have to face the actual act of doing so. But our willingness to give up that which is most precious to us is a good barometer of our "follower-ship" of Jesus. For, as long as we clutch tightly those things we hold precious, we can never open ourselves to the passionate embrace of our Savior.

What do you hold most dear? And are you willing to lose it for the embrace of your Savior?

It's easy to relate to the man who is asked to sacrifice everything. It's easy to sympathize with him. But if you were called to do the same, to radically commit your life to following Jesus, would you react any differently? I'd like to think I would. I'd like to think I could just say, "Here Jesus. Take it all." Some days, I think I'd be okay with that. Others, I think I'd have a hard time lettin' go.

Jesus calls for radical commitment, because the gift of salvation that he offers is radical. He gave his very life so that gift could be given to us. He's only asking that we give up some of our measly possessions. {sigh} "Oh, all right Jesus. Here ya go. But what do you *really* want with my Mystery Machine, stamp collection, and spork anyway?"

"Duh!" says Jesus. "I'm so sure! Scooby Doo rocks, man! And your stamps are kinda cool and I've been looking to trade some with Moses, and I know the spork story and I've been lookin' for one to use as a prop when I tell it!"

"Okay, Jesus. Fine. Take it all." I say in return with a little huff in my voice.

Jesus responds with a smile and twinkle in his eye and says, "Thanks, my friend. But why don't you keep your baby shoes. You'll need them as a reminder of how I'd like you to be when you show up asking to enter into my Kingdom." And then Jesus laughs. Not a mocking laugh—but a laugh of pure child-like Joy.

And I can't help but to laugh as well. He's gotten me. My Savior-friend has called forth the child within me and reminded me of the simple Joy that I once knew. And as I realize that Joy, I again see the twinkle in Jesus' eyes and I become aware of the Source of that Joy.

Baby steps, friends? Ah, heck, why not take a leap of faith?!

WE'VE GOT TO PRAY JUST TO MAKE IT TODAY

1 TIMOTHY 2:1

I get on a plane filled with people I don't know going places I can only imagine. I eat pre-packaged food with ingredients I don't want to know. I watch a movie which is semi-amusing. I read a book purchased at the airport convenience store. Nothing I would normally read, mind you, but something to pass the time. The plane crosses through two time zones and I end up in a strange airport, not knowing which direction to walk.

And so I begin to follow the crowd. I go where most people go. I end up at a place where I must choose where to go. I don't need to go with everyone else to the baggage claim, as I am a smart traveler and use only carry-ons. But this leaves me basically alone. So, I call my hotel and ask them how to get there. They tell me of the shuttle. I take it. I get to my room. And according to local time, it's already late by their standards. By mine, it's early morning. I'm tired. The sounds of the fluorescent lighting in the hotel lobby buzz at the fringe of my brain, giving me the feeling I'm in a Greyhound Bus Station at three in the morning.

Finally, I fall into my bed. The snores begin within moments. I'm certain my neighbors did not sleep as soundly as they had wished once I arrived. Either that, or their dreams were filled with the sounds of logs being sawed. Maybe my snoring caused them to dream of some madman with a chainsaw? The thought brings a smile.

Morning comes. What do my neighbors do first thing? Well, if they dreamed of what my snores may have caused them to dream, I'll bet they prayed first thing this morning! What did I do? Nothing so spiritual, I must confess. Nope. I located the coffee pot and brewed some...double strength, trying to rouse myself for the day and face it with some semblance of awareness.

What's the first thing you do each day? For me, I can honestly tell you that often I do not pray first thing. Often I hop into the shower, or take care of the dog, or brew some coffee. But this is changing. More and more, I'm remembering to say "Good morning" to God when I first realize consciousness. More and more...and when I do this, my day is usually very different from my coffee-first-thing mornings. On the days when I pray first, I've started my day, inviting Love to be at the center of it.

I didn't always know how to do this. I didn't always understand prayer.

Prayer seems so often to be just a time when we ramble on to God about the goings on of our day. Prayer is often just a list of "God blesses." To many, prayer is sometimes just a list of thank-yous. And to others, prayer is sometimes just a list of requests.

I think prayer is pretty illusive to most people. I think many people don't really understand what they're doing, how to do it, or even why they're praying. I think that many people feel like their prayers go unanswered and that prayer is more like a broadcast than a two-way radio, firing our requests randomly into the cosmos hoping that someone, somewhere will answer. We don't really expect an answer, do we?

Jesus prayed. He knew its importance. Regularly, Jesus got away from everybody, got down on his knees, and he prayed to his daddy. Yes, he did ask for things. But more than anything, Jesus listened for the will of God. He *expected* answers.

There is a difference between the prayers of our heads and the prayers of our hearts. The prayers which issue forth from our heads are logical, rational, and usually come off of some sort of a list. The prayers which bust out of our hearts are usually messy, unorganized, and are the cry of our souls. Our heart prayers are often unspoken. But when the words do come, they come unbidden...unlooked for...sometimes as a surprise. They spill forth in a jumble of emotional and soul-wrenching passion.

Head prayers are controlled. Heart prayers can't be controlled. Head prayers speak safely. Heart prayers speak dangerously. Head prayers lack feeling. Heart prayers drip with the sentiments of the soul. Head prayers assume a God who listens to copy down our list, bestow a cursory blessing, and then check that item off said list. Heart prayers assume a God who listens tenderly, who will sometimes say yes, sometimes no, sometimes wait, and sometimes that Grace must be sufficient. Head prayers are monotone. Heart prayers are harmonious and dissonant all at the same time. Head prayers are stoic. Heart prayers cry tears of sorrow and Joy.

Paul, in his letter to Timothy, tells Timothy that the first thing that he wants Timothy to do is pray. He doesn't just say this in a list of things that are important to do. He lists it as the first thing. In other words, it's of the highest importance. It is more urgent to pray than to do anything else. This is drop-everything kind of stuff. Before you preach, pray. Before you go there, pray. Before you eat, pray. Before you even get out of bed, pray. Before you do anything, pray. And pray from your heart. Let it go. Pray from the depths of your very soul. There is nothing to hide before God. God wants to have a relationship with you which goes beyond words on a list. God wants to know the struggles and the joys. God wants to reveal to you the difference Love can make in your life. If you keep praying with your head only, you will never hear the Voice of God, because God won't fit on to your list. If you start praying with your heart, you will come to know the Voice of Love and recognize when God is speaking to you of what Love will do for your life.

When you pray, realize that God indeed answers every prayer and like Jesus, expect answers. However, the answers are not always what we'd prefer. Then again, when has a life of faith ever been about what we *prefer*? I believe these are the four answers we receive from God when we pray:

"Yes. This is what is best for you, My child. And because you ask out of your faith, with a broken heart and pride, what you ask for shall be yours. I am glad to grant this request because I know that it is born of Love and blesses you."

"No. I'm sorry, although you may not be able to see it, this request isn't a good idea. It may be later. Or, it may never be, but for now, you're going to think I'm not answering. And that's because the answer is no." Garth Brooks sings a song which speaks directly to this: "Sometimes I thank God, for unanswered prayers. Remember when you're talkin' to the man upstairs, that just because he doesn't answer don't mean he don't care. Some of God's greatest gifts, are unanswered prayers."

"Wait. Not now. You're not ready. The situation isn't right yet. I have more things to prepare in your life. There are things you don't see...things you don't yet understand.

I need to fire you longer in my kiln to prepare you to withstand the pressures you must face." This is exactly the answer I received from God when I was praying to be sent to do a new church start. For almost two years, my answer to my prayers was "Wait."

The final answer God gives to us in prayer is: "My Grace is sufficient. I'm sorry to disappoint you, but there are times when obedience is all I ask. In some of these times, it will seem as if I'm not there. It will seem like I don't care or hear the cries of your heart. But in these times, all you need to know is that the Grace I have given to you in my son Jesus is sufficient...it's enough. Trust in it...trust in me. Be obedient. Submit your will to my Love. This is probably the hardest answer I will give to you in prayer, because it's ultimately about obedience...being obedient to me. You need to know that my grace is sufficient for you, My dear child. I died for you on the cross, and in the end, that will be enough because through that, you will receive my most precious gift, my Grace which will bring to you an eternity spent with me."

Pray today. Don't stop praying. Pray at work, in school, on the bus, in your car. Pray in the shower! Pray at meal times. Pray at bed times. Pray at all times. Pray. Pray hard. Pray soul prayers—heart prayers. Pray standing up. Pray sitting at your desk. Pray on your knees. Pray later. Pray right now.

And remember that so very much of prayer is listening.

What will this day hold for you, my dear friend? I have no idea...you have no idea. But God does. So why don't you talk to him about it?

THE SUBTLE DANGERS

2 PETER 2:1-2

For a couple of summers, I was a mud-boy for my older cousin, who was a tile-setter. It was my job to mix the mud (the cement) which was the foundation for the tile. It was my job to make sure that the mud was of the right consistency. It was my job to make sure that it had the right amount of moisture. It was my job to know the subtleties of the mud.

There were times when I made the mud too dry. And there were times when I made it too wet. At first, I couldn't tell the difference. And then my cousin showed me. He showed me perfect mud and what it is like to use as a foundation for the tile. And he showed me mud that was too wet and too dry and what it was like to use that for a foundation. Believe me, it makes a difference in how the mud sets and the type of foundation it becomes for the tile which will be set atop it.

But the differences are subtle, very difficult to detect with the naked eye.

In these days, there are teachers who are slightly off in some of their teachings to their congregations. The differences are subtle, difficult to detect with the un-trained, naked eye. The only way to be able to detect the differences between teaching that is right or wrong is to dig into the source of the teaching, the Bible.

And when Jesus was asked to sum up the Bible his answer was pretty straight forward: "Love God. Love people."

Basically, if it's Loving...do more of that. If it's not...knock it off.

If we put our only Hope in anything other than Love, then we are truly Hope-less.

And anyone teaching you to trust in anything besides Love, is leading you astray.

IN AWE OF BOB

PSALM 2:11

His face was red toned, gnarled, and had the appearance of a well-worn leather jacket, aged and creased. His long black hair was wound together in a braid. Work boots, Wrangler jeans, and a flannel shirt were his regular garb. At his waist, a large Bowie knife in a hand-tooled leather sheath. His bottom lip protruded from the bulge created by half a tin of "snus." And what one noticed after a while of being in his presence was that he never spit. He had a slight drawl to his low, rumbling voice. Curse words dotted the landscape of his vocabulary. He was intimidating, even a bit frightening, to be honest. One could never be certain of his words or actions.

Bob.

I remember the first time I met him at Franklin Elementary School in Anoka, Minnesota. Even though we were all afraid of him, we were fascinated at the same time. Maybe it was the large knife, or the casual way he replaced his snus, or the fluent profanity issuing forth from his mouth? Whatever the case, we were drawn to him like rubberneckers driving past a car accident, not wanting to see the details, but slowing down to look nonetheless.

"Boys, want some snus?" he'd regularly ask.

Mind you, I was about twelve at the time.

"Ummm...no thanks, Bob. That's gross."

"Alright boys, suit yourself."

I remember one time we screwed up our courage and asked him, "Bob, how come you swallow the juice from your snus?"

And through his gap-toothed, chew-stained grin he said these exact words: "Keeps the worms away, boys."

More than a couple of us had to swallow the bile forcing its way from our stomachs.

I'll never forget one campout at the Scout camp in Cannon Falls, Minnesota. It was Bob's first experience as a chaperone. And our first overnight experience with Bob. It was a bit like the feeling of going to a haunted house. You knew you were going to scared, but you went anyway and kind of liked it.

After a long day of hiking, quinzhee construction, sliding, and orienteering exercises in the snow searching for buried treasures of camping accoutrement created by Scoutmaster Jim utilizing map and compass, we retired to the cabin to make dinner and ultimately bed down for the evening.

Later on, Bob told us to go to bed in his own way, "Get in your fart-sacks, boys." And we did. We climbed into our sleeping bags.

After "lights out," we remained awake telling ghost stories, accepting truths or dares, and giggling like teenage boys do.

We were repeatedly "shushed" by our leaders. This happened many times over the course of two hours until finally somewhere slightly after midnight, after one particularly loud burst of laughter, Bob had had enough.

Do you remember the knife?

"God damn it! If you boys don't knock that shee-it off, I'm going to take my knife, shove it up your assholes, and then kick the handle off! Now shut the hell up, get in your fart-sacks, and go to sleep!"

We were all terrified, and yet laughing at the same time...on the inside. We weren't sure he was joking about the knife.

It is fascinating, is it not, that when we meet people of prominence: celebrities, dignitaries, CEOs, etc., we quite often stand in awe, fumbling for words, awkwardly trying to think of something clever to say so that we will impress.

And it was much like this when we faced Bob. We stood in awe of this man who laughed hard and loved life, and yet was a terrifying presence.

And yet, somehow we've lost this sense of God.

When we stand nose to nose with such, we are reminded of our place in all of this. However, when we stand there knowing we are loved, and responding with Love in return, our healthy fear is overcome by a sense of protection: of God being our refuge and our strength.

God is infinite, omniscient, omnipotence incarnate.

We should stand in awe of such. It should induce fear and trembling. It ought to bring us to our knees in humility.

In Psalm 2, it says this: "Serve the Lord with fear, and rejoice with trembling."

Serve with fear. Rejoice with trembling.

Serve God with a healthy sense of fear and awe, understanding that we are the created, and God is the Creator. But do not wallow in fear, becoming paralyzed from action. Do not seethe in bitterness arising from fear. Instead, rejoice. Yes, again I say, rejoice! Our sense of awe should remind us that we have an Almighty God who will never leave us and never forsake us. And it is in God...in God's Love...that we might find our refuge. It is in God that we would find shelter in God's wings. God has redeemed us by the power in the blood of Jesus who died for each of us.

Even Bob. Maybe even...*especially* Bob.

Tongue-Bump Diversions

Colossians 1:21-23

Argh. The pain. The agony. The madness of those darn little bumps that you get on your tongue. Do you know what I'm talking about? They're not canker sores. Although we often call them this. More than anything, they're just an inflamed taste-bud. What causes the inflammation? Who knows? A virus maybe? Too much sugar? A Canadian plot to win the Stanley Cup? I'm sure that someone learned who reads these musings may be able to let us in on the secret origin of tongue-bumps. If so, please email me!

All I do know, is they are maddening. Whenever I get these stupid things, they make me crazy. They are such a distraction. I'm sitting in a meeting with a fresh tongue-bump, rearing its ugly bud, and I just can't help moving my tongue around inside my mouth, dragging the bump over my teeth, feeling it go in and out of the grooves and spaces therein.

Occasionally, it would catch in a gap, and the peaceful flow of our meeting would be interrupted by a quiet little "Ouch" from me. I'm supposed to be focused...paying attention, for goodness' sake. Someone has put in hard work to prepare for this important meeting that I'm in so the least I can do is give them the respect of paying attention, right? All I know is that when you've got a tongue-bump, your attention span for anything beyond the bump itself is minimal. Until the bump has faded from your mind as well as your tongue, you will continue to be diverted and distracted.

I remember getting them as a kid. I would whine and complain to my parents. And they would either tell me to "quit crying or I would get something to cry about," or they would douse my tongue in Anbesol, helping me to speak with the grace of a dog with peanut-butter in its mouth. I remember when I got just a little older, like about ten years old or so. At about this age, my parents wouldn't dignify my whining with a response. If lucky, my mom would give me about this much sympathy: "Oh sweetie, I'm sorry...now go take out the garbage." Being a mature and responsible ten year old, I decided that I needed to take matters into my own hands. This problem needed to be taken care of, and I was going to have to be the one to do so.

I went to the bathroom. I stood in front of the mirror. I leaned in really close...so close, that my breath was fogging up the mirror. I stuck out my tongue. Aha! There's the culprit, I thought to myself. Now, what to do to rid myself of this evil? I opened the closet door in our bathroom. In there, one could find everything from hem-cool (Preparation H) to eyelash curlers, from baby aspirin to Old Spice. Some of the implements we had hiding in that closet would've been useful to Dr. Frankenstein himself. There were some scary items there. I was too afraid to ask about some of them. I rummaged through the bric-a-brac within: toothpaste? Nope, that'll make it sting worse. Hey, what about some hydrogen peroxide? It always seems to work on little cuts to clean them out. Maybe it'll help my tongue-bump?

Okay, dear friends, and trust me on this one, don't ever use hydrogen peroxide on your tongue. 'Nuff said.

I kept rummaging until I heard the angels singing *Hallelujah*, my hand came to rest on a pair of tweezers. Now, if you're squeamish, this is where you may want to close your eyes, because I'm guessing you might have an idea of what's coming next. With tweezers in hand, I returned to the mirror. I looked myself in the eye (you ever notice you can only look at one eye at a time?). There was a look of firm resolution and determination there. It was much the same look that Clint Eastwood has when he's Dirty Harry and is about to draw his guns on some unsuspecting cowboy who has double-crossed him.

With the look of Dirty Harry on my face, I steeled myself for what was to come. A tumbleweed blew by. I could hear someone whistling in a minor key off in the distance. My tweezer hand was gettin' itchy. It was time. I drew. I took the tweezers and grabbed for the tongue-bump. Zing. It slipped out of the tweezers. I tried again. Slip. By this time, I'm drooling all over the place, the pain in my tongue has gone from minor irritation to "Holy root canals, Batman!" I take a deep breath, calming my frayed nerves. I focus with the precision of a Zen master, wiping away the pain and all distractions from my sub-cortex. With a hand as steady as any bomb-squad expert about to clip the red wire, I take the tweezers, grab the tongue-bump, and pull...

I screamed. The kind of scream that you see in a movie when they have a camera shot from outer-space which has zoomed in on the house, and then pulls back to outer-space, indicating that the scream can be heard 'round the world. Blood gushed forth from my tongue. The pain was unfathomable. I would later know that only shark bites, kidney stones, and bullet wounds hurt worse than when you rip a tongue-bump from your being. It hurt, but the bump was gone. And with a little help from my dear friend Anbesol, a couple of Tylenol, and a few hours of time, the pain had subsided to a dull ache. By the next day, all I felt was a little tickly kind of pain around the site of the wound.

But the bump was gone. It was no longer a distraction to me. It no longer diverted my attention from the important matters at hand: like what was that girl's name sitting three desks up from me to the right?

Sometimes, we are distracted and our attention is diverted from what matters most. Tongue-bump diversions stealing our focus, erasing the thoughts which form at the tip of our mind. One minute, they seemed so very important, the next, our attention is diverted and we can only grasp at the fading protein trails, which almost had the chance to form in our brains to create a memory.

Paul writes to the Colossian church and in this passage, he reminds them of the tremendous gift we have been given through the death of Jesus. It was through the Cross and Jesus' death thereon, that God showed ultimate, extravagant, Untamed Love to us, and that our rebelliousness fades into the memories of yesteryear— that our very sins are forgiven. But we are too easily diverted from the true impact of this gift on our lives. Tongue-bump diversions, making the real gift of Jesus nothing more than a warm-fuzzy.

Sometimes, we must actually rip these distractions and diversions from our lives. There is no other solution. They won't just go away by themselves. They won't fade with time, or if they do, the damage to the rest of our lives will already be done. Sometimes, we must steel ourselves for some pain, take a deep breath, say a prayer, and then rip the tongue-bump diversion from our being, creating immediate pain, but in the midst of that pain, an incredible focus on the real and true things of life.

As long as we are diverted from the true impact of Love, we will never live as radical disciples, changing this very world through the power of God's Untamed Devotion. We will be, as I like to say, Diet-Coke Christians...just one calorie. We will not be the "real thing." We will be imitation disciples, looking good on the outside, but not having any real power or zing. Jesus will just give us a warm-fuzzy feeling, rather than cause us to be revolutionary agents of change in a hurting world. I believe that evil's greatest victory is convincing us that evil does not exist. But running a close second, is when evil is able to distract and divert us from the real impact of the gift that Jesus gave us on the Cross. For when we become distracted, we become children playing at church.

Do you want to play church? Or do you want to be revolutionary, radical, sold-out, Real Thing disciples? Do you want to be cheap imitations, packing Nerf-ball blows, bouncing off with little or no effect? Or do you want to LIVE Untamed lives, packing punches of power, changing this world by carrying a Message of even greater power to the least, the last, and the lost?

What distracts you from the real gift of Jesus, my friend? What diverts your attention from the wondrous gift of Love that was given through the Cross? What is making Jesus nothing more than a warm-fuzzy to you?

I suggest you pray about it, my dear friend. I suggest you ask for God's help in removing this diversion from your life. I suggest also, that it may be that nothing short of actually ripping every vestige of the diversion from your being may be exactly what you'll need to do. And know this: it'll hurt. But the hurt will fade. And you can use the pain to refocus yourself on Love. You can use the pain to re-energize your sense of urgency in sharing the Message. You can use the pain as a reminder of how you were diverted from that to which you were called on the day God's Love found you, my dear friend.

What diverts your attention from God's Love? And how will you rid yourself of the diversion?

I'm praying for you today. I'm praying for courage to face up to the reality of your diversions. I'm praying for strength to go through with the extrication of your diversions. And I'm praying for healing for you, for when you extricate the diversion, you will be wounded. And maybe the wound will only be in your pride. But that's okay...Healing is still available.

God Loves you. Big time. And showed that Love to you through the gift of Jesus' death on the Cross...a Love that is willing to give the ultimate sacrifice.

Do not be distracted and diverted from the real and true impact of that gift.

Mercy Walks...Repentance Runs

Luke 15:24

Lent is a time of reflection. It's a time when we look deep within ourselves and see what's lurking there. Sometimes we're surprised at how much garbage we've let build up. My friends, that garbage has a name. It's called sin.

Every time we head off on our own in life—every time we turn our backs on God—every time we sin, we're just like the son in the story. We've asked for our share of the inheritance up front and turned our backs on God. And inevitably, this leads us to a dark time in our lives.

It leads us to a time in our lives when we find ourselves getting ready to line up with the pigs at the trough. It's a crude, disgusting, and frightening image. We get to a point in the midst of our sin, where we're so entrenched within it, that we're not able to see a way out. We're not able to see, because we've built up a wall of pride around ourselves. And so, in the midst of our sin, we get down on our knees in the mud, next to the pigs, and then it hits us—*we don't have to live like this.* And the bricks in the wall of our pride come tumbling down and we're able to see the mess we've gotten ourselves into—and we're able to see that it's a mess we can't get ourselves out of. We realize we need help.

And so with heavy feet, and a heavy heart, we turn for home, dragging our feet because we realize how hard it will be to see our Daddy and admit to our foolishness. We're ashamed...and so in the midst of our repentance, we walk home.

Ah, but like the father in the story, our God will have none of this. From a distance, God sees us walking home. But our heavenly Daddy doesn't let us wallow in our shame. Instead, God is overjoyed that we've turned toward home—turned away from our sin—and God runs to meet us.

During this season of Lent, remember this: *Repentance walks...but Mercy runs.*

Falling Flat On Your Face

1 Corinthians 10:12

Often, when I need to make difficult decisions about life, I take a retreat. I go away at least for an afternoon, if not a day or two, and I just listen for God.

Most often, God speaks to me through metaphors. I am not one of those gifted with actual words which I hear from God. I have to listen with my eyes for what God is saying to me. Often, I instinctively know the answer to my difficult decision, but for whatever reason, am afraid to face up to it. Sometimes the fear is born out of the advice friends have given, because the metaphor which God gave to me spoke a different message than what my friends had to say. Fear, then, comes from the notion that God is asking me to go against what my friends have said. Other times, the fear is simply born out of the unknown, because the metaphor God has given requires me to travel off the map.

Here is one of the metaphors God gave to me one summer day while sitting on a fallen log, over a small river which runs through a small park in central Minnesota. I was facing a lot of confusion and indecision that day. I was questioning relationships and friendships. I was seeking God's guidance in what to do and say. That day, I knew the answer before I got to my place of retreat. But God, through a metaphor, spoke to me confirming this knowledge, goading me to action.

There is a squirrel with a twitchy-bushy tail that just ventured out onto a large tree which has fallen half-way across the river. It continues forth upon shakier and shakier branches, finally entrusting its weight to the tiniest of twigs. These tiny twigs splayed out towards the tiny twigs of another fallen tree on the other side of the river. If the squirrel wants to cross, it will have to jump into the air, grasping for the twigs of the other tree. As its tail twitches, it eyes the other branches, looking for a place to jump. Its haunches are tensed. It is ready. One quick breath and there...it made it. For an instant, the only thing which upheld the squirrel was the breath of God.

Right now God, I've been sitting on the tiniest of twigs. They barely support me. And yet, I must cross. I know You are leading me on to something. I don't know what, nor even where. But I know You are leading. And so I sit here trying to figure it all out, my own sense of balance, twitchy and bushy. And You are already on the other side.

"*Jump.*" You command.

"Why?" I ask.

"*Jump.*" Again, there You are, beckoning.

"Why?" I ask again, the consternation showing on my brow.

"*Because I said so,*" You say.

"Some answer."

"*But it's enough,*" You reply.

"Do I have to?" I ask.

"*If you want to be with Me,*" You say.

"But why can't You just stay with me?" I plead.

"*I will, but you need to move on...you need to go where I lead you.*"

I see Your eyes, solid, confident, filled with Love and power. Your arms outstretched to me as if to say: "It's okay. I'll catch you. Now jump."

I take a deep breath, my muscles become taut and flex as I launch myself into the air. I wave my arms crazily as I realize that I can't make it. And I realize then, that in You, I am being borne upon the open space by Your Breath. It strikes me then, that there was never really a gap. The gap was only in my mind.

I sense the openness before me.
And yet I know You're always there.
The gap I see an illusion.
Your Breath will bear me through the air.
The Breath of God,
My Breath of Life.
The Breath I breathe,
You give New Life.
On the Breath of God,
I take my stand.
You look to me,
With outstretched hands.
Oh Breath of God,
You sing to me.
On You I stand,
In You I'm free.
Your outstretched hands,
I see Your scars.
No heart-born wish
Upon the stars
Will carry me
Always, ever on,
As You carry me,
Oh Breath of God.

What decisions do you face today? Have you sought out the Voice of God regarding your decisions? Have you really taken time out to listen?

Next question: in whom are you trusting? Are you trusting solely in your own power to choose? Are you seeking wise counsel? Or are you trusting in God's Love? If you only trust in yourself, inevitably, there will come a time when you will fall flat on your face. And it will be painful, embarrassing, and pride-crushing.

But then again, maybe you need that. Maybe you need to have your pride crushed? I know that on many occasions, this is exactly what the doctor has ordered for me. A nice fall-on-my-face to remind me of my place. A reminder that God is God, and *I am not.*

Paul, in his letter to the church in ancient Corinth, tells us to cultivate *God*-confidence. Trust in Jesus. Know that his very Breath will you hold up when you trust in his Love and leap from the paltry branch that strains under your weight.

As long as you trust only in yourself for your major decisions, you will occasionally fall flat on your face.

When you trust in God for your major decisions, you will always see his Love reflecting on your face.

Falling flat on your face, or having the very Love of God reflecting upon your face? Hmmm...tough decision.

For it is only by a leap of faith that you will discover flight.

DO YOU GET IT?

JOHN 13:2-8

Calculus was almost the death of me. I was in advanced mathematics courses all the way through middle school, junior high, and then into senior high. First there was algebra in 8th grade, geometry in 9th, higher algebra in 10th, elementary functions (trigonometry and pre-calculus) in 11th, and then, the crème de la crème of high school math: calculus.

Mr. Swenson was our teacher. And truly, he wasn't really a teacher. He was a purveyor of information. He was a college professor who would come to the slums...er ah, to our high school and teach one course. Just one. Calculus.

Ugh.

He would walk with the dignity of a British lord as he marched into our classroom. We met just a couple of times each week for one hour. He looked rather like Sir Winston Churchill. Mr. Swenson was a bit pompous and aloof. To this day, I don't know if he came to our class to convey information from on high or to inflict great pain. Maybe it was a combination of the two. Out of a classroom of twenty-three teenagers, maybe two really wanted to be there. I'll bet you had them in some of your classes as well. They're the ones who actually could speak Klingon, knew the limitations of dilithium crystals, and could tell you the maximum velocity which could be reached on "impulse power."

They loved math. And not only did they love math, but they adored calculus and they got it. While I got the concept and big picture of calculus, I never fully grasped its practice.

I'll never forget that class. Because as each day in Mr. Swenson's class would go by, it seemed another person would get it. You could almost see the lightbulb turning on over each person's head as they got it.

Sadly, not everyone did. I managed a passing grade. But the lightbulb moment never came for me.

I didn't get it.

Neither did Peter.

Over and over, the disciples just don't get it. They're standing right next to the Savior of the Universe and they don't get it. Daily they're walking with the One who created the Universe and they don't get it.

They're with *God*. And they don't get it.

There are times when I read these passages and I think "duh!" How do you not see who this is? How do you not see Jesus for Who he really is?

I think it had to do with the fact that maybe God wasn't done revealing Who he was. There was more that needed to be shown to the disciples so they could tell the world...so they would be motivated to tell the world and not just a few of their buddies. One of the final revelations to the disciples happens in this scene.

Jesus wants to show his disciples the true heart of his father...his *Daddy*. That's the word Jesus used: *Abba*. And the best translation of that is *Daddy*. It's so tender. Intimate. And Jesus wants the disciples to see that. He wants to show them his Servant heart. He wants to show them Love.

Here, we see God as the Ultimate Servant.

In this scene, we see the Almighty God, humbling himself before his friends to serve them. The Omnipotent God sets aside the Majesty we think of when we think of God, and redefines the word. True majesty is to serve out of a heart of Love. But Peter doesn't want this. He doesn't want Jesus to serve him because he doesn't see himself as worthy. Because Peter, of all the disciples, was the one I think came the closest to getting it. He had a glimpse. Peter went to the mountain top with Jesus and saw him shine with bright light. Peter walked on water with Jesus. Peter had an inkling of Jesus' divinity and thus felt unworthy to receive the gift of his service. But unless Peter experiences what it is like for God to serve him, he will never be a part of the great works of God. Because for God, it's all about a servant heart.

If you can right now, take off your shoes and socks and take a look at your feet. Feet are kind of weird. We keep them covered up all of the time. We hide our feet from the world. They're smelly. They're funny shaped. They're even kind of embarrassing. Most of us are pretty ticklish on the bottom of our lowest appendages. Feet seem sort of silly, and at the same time, there is an intimacy which is associated with our feet. I think this intimacy is part of the point. Because servanthood is intimate. *God's Love* is *intimate*.

Now close your eyes and imagine Jesus kneeling in front of you. He kneels there all-mighty, all-knowing. As he kneels in front of you, he sees the depths of your heart in this moment. He knows with what you struggle today. He knows the burdens you have been carrying. He knows the sins you've tried to hide. He knows the wounds out of which those sins come. He knows the shame you bear. He *knows*...and yet there he is, kneeling before you, this Almighty God, King of All Kings, Savior of the Universe—

there he is, kneeling to serve you. He wants to wash your feet. How does it make you feel to know that God would kneel before you and wash your feet? Does it humble you? Does it shame you?

I must confess to feeling both of these. I feel humbled to know that God loves me this much. But I also feel ashamed because I know that I have not knelt nearly enough at the feet of others to serve them. And in this, I deny the true nature of God.

This Servant knelt in the dust to wash your feet, and then rose and carried our sin and shame upon the cross. He made our feet clean to show us the heart of the Father...of his *Daddy*. He made our hearts clean upon the cross so that we will know that same Untamed Love.

God was willing to kneel at the feet of his children to teach them to kneel before others. God was not just willing to do this...he had to, because, after all, that's Who he is.

If the occasion were ever to arise, I would with all humility, kneel before Mr. Swenson and wash his feet. An unlikely event...to be sure. But wouldn't it be just like Jesus to make it come about? That'd be pretty cool.

God bless you, Mr. Swenson. I hope I have the opportunity to serve you someday.

The Rest of Holy Week

Matthew 21:17-18

Each year, when we celebrate Holy Week, we always start by reading the Scripture of Jesus' triumphal entry into Jerusalem. Then we skip to reading about the Last Supper with his disciples. Then we read the texts about the crucifixion. And then we're off to Easter Sunday.

What about the rest of the week? What about Monday, Tuesday, and Wednesday of that week? What did Jesus' do? What did he say? Where did he spend his time? What were his priorities?

Chapters 21-26 of Matthew are great reading. Much of Jesus' teachings are found in these passages. Much of the core of his teaching on the Kingdom of God, the hypocrisy of the Pharisees, and who goes to Heaven and who goes to Hell is found in these few chapters. I think it's some of his boldest teaching. It certainly ticked off the religious leaders.

There is urgency in this time. You can sense it. I imagine Jesus going from place to place, rushing. Maybe for the first time in his ministry, Jesus hurried. He knew that his time was short. He still had much to teach with little time left. He was helping his disciples cram for their final. He wanted to make sure they knew who he was, why he came, and what to watch out for. He told them they would be persecuted. He even suggested who would do it. He told them that some will go to Heaven and some will go to Hell. He prophesied about the day when he would come again to judge the living and the dead. This was a powerful time of ministry for Jesus...and yet we gloss over it each year when we read the story of Holy Week.

I challenge you today to read these chapters. Learn. Learn what was important to Jesus in the last days of his ministry. Much of this stuff is the core of his teaching. Watch for the heart of God in these pages. Discern God's will for your life in these pages. See through Jesus' eyes. Pray with him. Feel his urgency. Be inspired by it. Take this sense of urgency with you to the Last Supper this Thursday. Take this urgency with you to the cross on Friday. Take it with you to the empty tomb on Sunday. And take this urgency with you to wherever you are at this moment. Do not let the urgency that Jesus felt in his last days of ministry fall upon deaf ears. Take that urgency with you into this world which needs to know about Jesus.

LIFE'S SHORT, PRAY HARD

LUKE 22:39-44

How hard do you pray? I'm not asking how often. I'm not even asking simply how you pray. I'm asking how *hard* do you pray? Really. If we're grading on effort here and not the actual product, how would you score?

I used to be an apprentice to my cousin who is a tile-setter. Tough job. The main part of my job was to "mix mud." Basically, I was given a huge, crusty tub, a hoe, some 5-gallon buckets, gallons upon gallons of water...and pallets stacked with bags of cement. It was my job to place 3 bags of cement into the tub, add about 3 1/2 to 4 gallons of water, and then use that hoe to chop the water into the cement. I had to go the length of the tub 3 times to properly mix the water in with the cement mix turning it into "mud." I was to then use the hoe to scoop the mud into the 5-gallon buckets, which I then carried over planks into the house. Each bucket weighed about 50 pounds. And there were five, 5-gallon buckets full of cement per batch. A light day of work was around 20 to 30 bags of cement which comes out to be about 7 to 10 batches, which means about 35 to 50 5-gallon buckets full of cement, which comes out to be around 1,750 to 2,250 pounds.

That was a light day. On light days, I perspired.

On the heavy days, I moved around 80 to 100 bags of cement. One hundred bags comes out to be about 33 batches, which is 165 buckets full of mud, equaling 8,250 pounds. On heavy days, I sweated. On heavy days, I was working hard. And it showed.

In this passage from Luke, we find Jesus soon after he has shared his last meal with his disciples. He feels the weight of what is coming. It's obvious in this passage that Jesus is kind of hoping for another way...a way out. But it is in this passage, that we see his obedience to his *Daddy*. It is in this passage, that we see Jesus wrestling with what is about to come. It is in this passage, that we see Jesus praying so hard, that he not only sweats...but it appears as if he is sweating blood.

What could cause a person to sweat like this? Have you ever sweated like this? Have you ever carried such a burden, that you sweated blood? What could cause this?

Maybe carrying the weight of the sins of the world? Maybe knowing all of the wounds of all of the people's hearts that made those sins possible? Maybe knowing that a crown will be fashioned from some vines with inch-long thorns and it will be shoved down around your brow, gouging into the flesh of your scalp? Maybe knowing that you will be whipped until the skin of your back is not only bloodied, but torn...ripped apart?

Maybe knowing that you will carry the cross to which you will be nailed? Maybe knowing that your best friends will deny you and watch you be nailed to that cross? Maybe knowing that rough, rusty iron spikes will be driven through the tendons and bones of each of your wrists...that another crusty spike will force its way through the bones and flesh of your ankles, driven by a huge mallet and the force of a muscular Roman soldier as others stand by and laugh? Maybe knowing that when you finally die of asphyxiation on that cross, you will have to descend into Hell itself to wage a war against the power of Satan on behalf of all of humanity?

Maybe this knowledge is what caused Jesus to pray so hard. He knew what he would face. He knew that the only strength he had came from his Daddy. He knew that to face the onslaught of the forces of Hell, He would need the glory-strength which would come from deep prayer—communication with his Daddy.

My friends, each day, we need this same kind of prayer. Because of the sacrifice Jesus made that day on the cross, we will never have to descend to Hell if we trust in God's Love. We will never have to wage a one-on-one battle with Satan on his home turf. But we still wage a one-on-one battle each day on our turf. God calls out to us constantly to pray—to talk with him and listen, because God knows that our only strength, our only hope against evil is the glory-strength that comes through Love.

Imagine today is a 20-bag-day of prayer. It's some work, but it's pretty easy. You don't need to try that hard. The prayers will prayed. You may perspire. Your work will get done. Bada-bing...bada boom.

But that's not the case. Every day, a spiritual war is being waged for your soul. Every day is a 100-bag day of prayer. You need to pray hard. Imagine praying so hard that you sweat. Now imagine praying so hard that you actually sweat blood. This is the intensity with which Jesus prayed that day. He prayed that hard, because he Loves us...He Loves you, my friend.

Praise God that Jesus did pray that hard...praise God that Jesus knelt in the garden that day, humbling himself before his Daddy...submitting his will. Thank God today, that Jesus knew from where his strength would come, so that he could fight the battle he fought. Because if he had not...if he had only relied on his human strength, then our sins would not be forgiven. Thank God that Jesus prayed hard.

His life was short. He prayed hard. The battle was fought and won. Our sins are forgiven each time we look at the cross and remember what Jesus has done...each time we spend time in God's Love.

Life is short...pray hard, my friend.

Please Stay, Judas!

John 12

I heard someone say recently that they wished that Judas would have left after this. They wished that Judas would have been cast by Jesus from his presence.

I don't. I want Judas to stay. Maybe if he stayed, he would see? Maybe if he stayed, he would see the heart of Mary and understand her devotion? Maybe if he stayed, he wouldn't have to betray?

My heart breaks for Judas. What a lonely man...a lost man. He finds his value only in the coins in his purse. The gleam of silver was brighter to him than God's Love.

The sheen of silver blinded him to God's Grace.

Judas walked with Jesus. He talked with him. He ate with him and probably even slept next to him. And yet Judas still didn't understand who Jesus was. There was something in Judas that Jesus saw as worthy of being his disciple. Was it simply his ability to care for the finances of their band of disciples? Was it simply his organizational ability? The Lord knows we need good administrators in this world. But was that why Judas was chosen?

Or was Judas chosen because Jesus knew he would stay blind to God's Love? Was Judas chosen precisely because he would be blinded by silver to the Love of God because Jesus knew the path he would have to trod. Or did Jesus hope until the last moment in the Garden that Judas' heart would be changed?

I want Judas to stay...because we have all been Judas. We have all been in the presence of God and have been blinded to Love by the sheen of earthly things. We have all walked next to God and not recognized him. We have all had our hearts in the wrong places, blind to the Right Place...the Heart of God.

Don't ever hate Judas. Don't curse him. Don't judge him. Instead, pity him. Because we have all been him. And just like Judas, we all have our wounds. For it is out of our woundedness that we sin. Pray today, that the sheen of earthly things would be dulled so that you would see God's Love. Make this your prayer.

Remember the old hymn:

Amazing Grace, how sweet the sound, that saved a wretch like me (like Judas). *I once was lost, but now am found, was blind, but now I see.*

Lord, I praise You today for being able to see You and not being blind to Your Love. Amen.

No Other Name

Acts 4:5-12

I went to seminary (pastor school) in Chicago. We left behind all of our friends and family to move to the breezy city to pursue my education. Probably one of the most difficult aspects of this was that we left behind our loved ones. And it wasn't all that easy to meet new people. Chicagoans don't quite understand the term "Minnesota nice." I was often lonely and missed my friends.

So, one day when I was home taking care of my infant son and I got a phone call out of the blue from some incredibly friendly person, it should come as no surprise that I was a bit eager to have contact with a friend. At least on the telephone, she seemed like a friend. She seemed to know things about me. She knew that I was studying to be a pastor. She knew of my son. She knew stuff about home and friends and family.

She called and said "Hi, Shane! It's Lisa!"

"Great," I thought, "who's Lisa?" So, I was racking my brain, trying to figure out with whom I was speaking. You ever do that? Someone calls you and you can tell they know you, but you don't know them? And suddenly you become a private detective, using the Sherlock Holmes' method of deductive reasoning to eliminate all of the wrong answers to find the right one.

"So, how's your family?" you ask, hoping they'll reveal a crucial bit of information which will clue you into their identity.

"Just fine." they answer. With a vague answer like that, you don't know if they're married or not. They could be talking about their parents and siblings, for that matter.

"So...how's work?" you ask, thinking they'll say the name of their employer or something and then you'll know who they are.

And you get lucky, they do say the name of their employer, "Working for Kraft Foods has been good to me." they say. But as far as you are aware, you have no friends who work for Kraft Foods.

And so the conversation went. Me asking questions trying to figure out with whom I was speaking. Her answering them thinking she's having this great conversation with someone who knows her so well.

Not that any of *you* have this issue, but occasionally I have issues with pride. I would rather die some days than end up looking stupid. I know. Stupidity or death...and I choose death. Yup, that's intelligent. So, rather than look stupid while talking to "Lisa," I just kept pretending like I knew who she was. I figured we'd end up having a great conversation and she'd tell me to say hi to my family...and then we'd amiably say "goodbye." My plan was going perfectly right up until the point where she asked me if we could all get together sometime.

"Sure!" I said. Thinking that was a rather noncommittal response because most people say this but don't actually follow through with it.

She did.

"How about Saturday?" she asked.

"Saturday?" I said choking.

"Yeah, Saturday. What would you like me to bring?" she asked.

"Uh...dessert, I guess."

"Okay, I'll see you Saturday night. What time should I come over?"

"Six o'clock?" I said somewhat falteringly.

"Great! See you then." Click.

Soon after, my wife called me up to see how things were going. And I responded by asking her who we were having over for dinner.

"You mean, you don't know who you invited over for dinner?" she asked in a way which let me know that the translation of her statement meant something like: "Sadly you have a brain the size of a pea and are a rather slow-witted beast without any excuse for polluting the gene pool. You are the weakest link. Good bye."

"Uh..." I said rather profoundly, trying to feign dignity, "nope." I said.

And I had no idea who was coming to dinner until I opened our door, Saturday at six o'clock.

Not knowing her name caused me a bit of grief over the next few days. The lack of this knowledge had power over us.

Names carry inherent power.

And so when Peter and John were being questioned by the Chief Priest and other religious leaders about what they were doing and in whose name they were doing it, what they were really being asked about was the power and authority behind the name.

Peter, very boldly stood to tell them all that day, "It's in the name of Jesus that we do what we do. And you know what, there's no other name that can even come close to the power and authority of this name. Because there's no other way for you to be saved from sin and death, than through this name. So wake up folks."

Names have power. Lots of it. Names have caused people to die. Names have caused slavery. Names have caused genocide. Names have built kingdoms. Names have brought Joy.

A name on a book, or a painting, or a tombstone, or even a name on an item of clothing...all of these hold power. Recently, a young man was killed, not because of a gang war or because he had done something wrong. He was killed because someone wanted his name brand tennis shoes. Someone took a life in the name of shoes. These names have power. And these names I speak of here are only mortal names.

The name of Jesus is immortal and eternal and carries with it the power of immortality and eternity. There is no other name by which we are saved than the name of Jesus.

What's your name? Think of the power inherent in your name. When people know your name, they know a great deal about you. This name identifies you. In a crowd of people, if someone shouts your name, they have caused a reaction within you. You turn and look to see who speaks this word which has such power to make you move. When you were a child and got lost in a crowd and you heard your mommy or daddy yelling your name, think of the joy and relief you felt when you heard it. If a policeman were to knock on your door at three in the morning and ask if you were who you are...that simple utterance of your name identifies you as the receiver of whatever news the policeman heralds. Your stomach sinks as they say your name and then say they're sorry. Think of how your name is used. Think of the power in your name. Think of how people use, abuse, and misuse your name.

And now think of the name of Jesus. Say it. Say his name right out loud. Feel the power there? Do you feel how it resonates as you speak it? Say his name...no, proclaim it! And as it echoes around you throughout eternity, know the ultimate power in that name: the power over sin and death.

Because you see, my dear friend, this name you have just spoken, is the only name which can save you from yourself. It is the only name which has the power to do so. No other name can even come close.

By the way, her name was *Elisa*. Not Lisa. And we knew her well. She was a part of my youth group from my old church and she had moved to Chicago and had looked me up. One letter made a huge difference. It changed her name from something which had no meaning and no power to something with great power: the power of recognition and memory and friendship.

Think of names today. Think of their power. Think of how you use them. And think as well about how you use the name of Jesus. Do you use it? Do you abuse it? Do you misuse it? I'm quite certain I've done all three.

I don't like it when people abuse or misuse my name.

I'm guessing God's not so much a fan of this either. But I'm also guessing God understands and Loves us anyway.

GOD IN A BOX

1 CORINTHIANS 10:14

Have you ever had a little bout of insomnia and gotten caught up in an infomercial? They often sell stuff that in your right mind, you would never even consider purchasing. But, at 2 in the morning, it's amazing what you can be convinced of. Because pretty soon, you find yourself not only thinking that you just may need the worthless piece of junk being sold...but that if your credit card were only handy...oh yes...the worthless piece of junk would be yours...

...yours for only 3 easy payments of $19.95, plus shipping and handling.

I think this is exactly the kind of God which is often marketed these days. A God who exists only to satisfy our needs. A God who is there when we need it...and we can fold God up and put him away when we're done...because he's handy and easily storable underneath our beds or in a closet. There are churches that market this kind of a God. They will tell you that if you only speak the word of faith, then whatever it is your heart desires will be yours. This is the genie-in-a-bottle God. Believe in him and your wishes will be granted.

Other churches tell us that God simply exists to fill the needs of the needy. They will tell you that God is a God of social justice and if we would all just fall in line and march to the cadence of their creed, then God's Kingdom will come and his will be done.

This is the we-really-don't-need-a-God-if-we-make-the-right-choices God...but let's have a God anyway and we will call him Justice.

Other churches will tell you that God exists only when we gather to worship him. They will tell you that God just wants to hear of how great he is and when we tell him, we will be blessed. This is the I-like-to-hear-the-sound-of-my-name-God.

These viewpoints espouse a God of convenience.

God in a box.

Now, don't get me wrong...God does fulfill our needs—when our needs match up with his Love. God does desire justice—but out of his Love. God does desire our worship—not to hear the sound of his name, but to feel the Love in our hearts.

God exists whether we have needs or not. God exists whether we make right choices or not. God exists whether we worship him or not. God is the Alpha and the Omega...the Beginning and the End. God was. God is. And God always will be...whether we will be or not. God's existence does not depend on ours. And God most certainly isn't always convenient.

When God, through Jesus, called to Andrew and Simon (who became Peter...the founder of the Christian church!) from their fishing, God wasn't all that convenient. When God called Levi (who became Matthew) from the riches of collecting taxes, asking him to give it all back...God wasn't all that convenient. When God called his son Jesus to show his Love by dying a violent death on a cross...God wasn't being convenient.

God calls each of us today...and friends, God isn't being convenient about it. He calls us out of sin...out of our woundedness. God calls away from behaviors which do not show Love. God calls us to his Love wherever and whenever we are: in our workplaces, in our homes, in the mall, in the sports club, in the bar, at school...and hopefully in our churches as well. God calls us to use our money in ways which show Love as well.

No, God isn't very convenient. But then again...he's God. God isn't a jack-in-the-box we wind up and expect to pop up to entertain our every whim.

Paul writes this to the church in Corinth. Apparently there were people there who believed in a God you could put into a box, Who existed only to serve our needs, instead of the other way around. Paul's advice to this church is sound: "when you see people reducing God to something they can use or control, get out of their company as fast as you can."

May we never reduce God to our convenience.

God, we Love You even when it's not convenient. We will show Your Love...especially when it's not convenient. We will rely on Your Love in our lives to make the right choices...and not simply rely on our own power to choose. God, thanks for the reminder today from Your servant Paul...that it ain't all about us...it's all about Your Love! We love You! Thanks for breaking into the tidiness of our lives to remind us of Your inconvenience...because in doing so, You remind us of how very much we are Loved. Amen.

Easter Grass Reminders

1 Corinthians 15:12-20

The hubbub of Easter has died down. The baskets are put away. Most of the candy has been consumed. There are still vestiges of the celebration around our home, mostly in the form of the annoying plastic Easter grass which has infiltrated our carpet. Easter grass is persistent. It clings to stuff with static electricity. It wheedles its way into the carpet making it sometimes difficult for the vacuum cleaner to extract. To truly remove the stuff, you need to get a pair of tweezers, lay down and look at the carpet at ant-level, and begin to go through your house, covering every square-inch. Either that or hook up a v-8, 400 cubic-inch engine to your vacuum cleaner that'll suck the dirt from your basement right up through the floor. Easter grass is nigh impossible to entirely remove from your house. And just last night, as I was doing the laundry, I found a clump of the stuff in the dryer.

Easter grass is an annoying reminder of a blessed event.

First, we need to acknowledge what an "event" is. An event is something which has happened. Anything which happens is an event. An event, as something that has happened, is factual history.

Easter happened a few weeks ago. We celebrated Jesus conquering sin and death for all time. We celebrated the empty tomb. We celebrated an event which happened almost two thousand years ago. We celebrated the force of Love in this world that provides us Hope.

And now, a few weeks later, when we're beginning to focus on summer, cabins, lakes, no school, vacations, and yard-work, we're still finding Easter grass around the house. Can't we ever get rid of this stuff?

I hope...no, I pray not. Because I need reminders. I need to be reminded of the Via Dolorosa...the way of suffering and blood that Jesus walked on that Friday so long ago. I need to be reminded of the crown of thorns pushed so mockingly onto his head. I need to be reminded of the crude spikes driven through the flesh of my Savior. I need to be reminded of his last words: "It is finished." And I need to be reminded that the story did not end there.

I need to be reminded of Easter...an event that happened.

Because if it did not, then Jesus was a lunatic or just a great moral teacher. And either way, we're left with nothing in which to Hope but ourselves and our own power to make good choices. I don't always have a lot of faith in humankind's ability to make good choices. Every time I turn on the news, I see less and less of a reason for humankind to hope in its power to choose for the good.

Here's the plain and simple truth: if Jesus was not raised from the dead, then our faith is a sham.

No, Jesus Christ must be more than a myth, more than simple inspiration, more than a great moral teacher. For our faith to mean anything, Jesus must be exactly who he said he was:

the Son of God, one with the Father,

Who will come again someday,

Who drove out demons,

Who healed the sick,

Who raised the dead,

Who walked on water,

Who turned water into wine,
Who fed the hungry,
Who ate with sinners in their own homes,
Who wept,
Who prayed,
Who was tempted,
Who got angry,
Who rejoiced,
Who broke bread saying "Take this, all of you and eat, for this is My body which is broken for you,"
Who died on a cross...
Who was raised from the dead.

And who showed the greatest Love of all: he gave up *his* Life so that *we* might LIVE.

Paul says it: "But the truth is that Christ HAS been raised up..." It happened. It was real.

And the Easter grass which is still in your house somewhere is a reminder!

Passing the Test

1 Thessalonians 2:3-5

Mr. Jorgensen was his name. He was our third scoutmaster. Our first one was old and his sons had grown so he retired from being our scoutmaster. Our second one was simply inept and knew it, so left behind being a scoutmaster rather quickly. And then there was Jim.

James H. Jorgensen. He even had a cute way of putting the three initials all together JHJ. This monogram adorned every possible item which belonged to him, from his tooth brush to his sleeping bag—JHJ everywhere. I often wondered if he had this monogram tattooed somewhere on his body...just in case.

Mr. Jorgensen took scouting very seriously. For the sake of Pete, this man carried a whistle around his neck. He stopped just short of wearing fatigues and camouflage paint on his face. And while camping, he would rouse us each morning by sticking his head into our tents and blowing that God-forsaken whistle. Have you ever been awakened by a whistle blown by an obnoxious Italian man at 6AM? I challenge you to retain your patience. I defy you to remain sane. There were many times when we spent serious hours plotting fiendish tortures for Mr. Jorgensen. Because while he was like General MacArthur, we were more like the soldiers from *Stripes*.

"Hey, were you kids mocking me?" he would ask.

"That's a fact, Jack!" we'd shout like good soldiers.

Let's just say that our relationship was strained. But for all that Mr. Jorgensen was somewhat of a caricature of a scoutmaster, he had many redeeming qualities. Because he took Scouting so seriously, our scout troop went on adventures that many troops do not. We backpacked through the Rocky Mountains in New Mexico. We went sailing on a 40-foot sailboat on Lake Superior with 7-foot waves. We went rock climbing and rappelling. We went winter camping and built snow-shelters called quinzhees and slept in them.

And because Mr. Jorgensen took scouting so seriously, he also took the testing for our merit badges and other awards very seriously. The only thing that really compares is passing the bar exam or medical boards, or maybe walking over hot coals barefoot while juggling chainsaws and singing an aria from *Swan Lake*. He tested us.

One of the tests he took most seriously was the one for getting what was called our Totin' Chip. A Totin' Chip is what entitles a scout to carry or "tote" a pocket knife. To receive this coveted piece of paper, you had to learn everything from knife etiquette to knife care, all the uses of your scout knife, to the history of pocket knives being used by boy scouts. If you could run the gauntlet of Mr. Jorgensen's Totin' Chip Ordeal, you had achieved greatness. Because you had been tried, tested, and found worthy to carry a knife.

Paul, the guy who wrote our Scripture for today, I think was probably quite a bit like Mr. Jorgensen. He took Jesus and faith very seriously. As Mr. Jorgensen was zealous in scouting, Paul was zealous in his faith. Paul speaks in this passage of being tested by God and found worthy or qualified to bear the Message of Jesus Christ. And truly, Paul was tested. He was beaten, robbed, imprisoned, whipped, shipwrecked, starved, and almost killed. He traveled literally thousands of miles to carry the Message to people who had never heard. He sacrificed the thing most precious to anyone for the sake of the Message...his pride. This sacrifice was probably the greatest test he underwent. Even greater than all of the torture and imprisonment was his willingness to set himself aside.

It is only by setting ourselves aside...by sacrificing pride, that we are able to share the Message without seeking glory for ourselves. For if we do not set aside pride, the Message is still the Message, but we preach it for human approval. And when we do that, we soften the import of the Message so we will not be offensive. When we care about human approval ratings, we will take care not to offend. And in doing so, we fail the test miserably.

I have failed this test, to be sure. There have been times when I have softened the blow of the Message so that I would attain the approval of the crowd. And in doing so, I found only the disappointment of God, and the Message becomes something other than what God's Love is about. When I have sought crowd approval and preached a wussy message, I have not preached the Message. I have put Jesus aside. I have denied him just as Peter did. I have failed the test.

But here is the difference between Jesus and Mr. Jorgensen: *Grace.*

Unmerited favor, undeserved forgiveness, unwarranted second and third and ninety-third chances. Because God Loves us.

Friends, ultimately it comes down to this: we have two choices to make. Do we seek crowd approval or God's approval? If we seek crowd approval, we may have our friends and family look upon us favorably. But in doing so, we deny God. For if you pass the test, seeking only God's approval and are entrusted with the Message, someday you will stand before the Throne of Heaven and

Jesus will select you out of the line-up of the ages, look into your eyes with pride and say "Good job, my friend. You've done well. I'm proud of you."

When we pass the test...when we lay ourselves aside for the sake of the Message, we are then able to carry or "tote" the Message to those who need to hear it. And not some wussy-version of it. No, the real thing! As Scouts, we didn't want to carry wussy-knives. We wanted real knives. But to carry them, we had to pass the test.

To set aside our pride is difficult. But in doing so, God authorizes us to tote the Message of Love to the least, the last, and the lost. And dear friends, the gift of God's trust to carry the Message is more precious than any treasure. I will not soften the Message and make it wussy. Because not only does that cheat our Savior, but it cheats those who need its saving power.

I would take a thousand jeers from my friends...for one look of pride from God. I would endure the taunts of those dearest to me to hear one person say after they've heard the Message: "I Love you, Jesus."

By the way, in Heaven, we'll not be awakened by whistles. Nope...that's the other place.

THE DEFENSE NEVER RESTS

1 JOHN 2:1

The gavel is slammed down three times in rapid succession. The shock of the curt report of the hammer-shaped piece of wood striking the Judge's bench jars you from your thoughts. "This court will come to order."

You stand in a courtroom. Imagine the rich wood of the Judge's bench. Look up and see the face of the Judge. His face gives away nothing. You see neither mercy nor condemnation yet written there. You look around the courtroom.

On one side, you see the Accuser. He's the prosecutor. He's filing charges against you. It is being alleged that you have committed sins. It is being alleged as well, that your faith was empty and wasted. Satan, the Accuser, turns to look at you. You see a glint in his eye. He's got evidence against you. It's written in his eyes for all to see. You are guilty. Satan sneer's at you with his self-satisfied smug smirk. You begin to recount the evidence in your mind. And you realize with shame, that everything he says that you have done or not done is absolutely true. You stand there, head hung with the weight of your guilt.

Again, you hear the voice of the Judge, "How does the defendant plead?"

You begin to mutter and say, "Guil..."

But there is a commotion coming from the back of the courtroom. A man is walking down the aisle toward you. He's kind and gentle looking. And yet, there is a quiet strength within this man. You can sense there is something more to him than meets the eye. Your muttered attempt at a plea is cut off as the Man walks toward you and says "Guilty, Your Honor...but there are extenuating circumstances of which this court needs to be made aware."

Your mouth hangs open...incredulous. Who is this man? Why does he change the nature of your plea? What evidence does he have of which you are not aware? You are certain that you are guilty of everything of which you are accused. How can this be?

The Accuser raises an objection, "I object, Your Honor. I was not made aware of a Defending Attorney for this trial. I respectfully ask that this Man be removed from these proceedings."

The Judge, with justice written on his face, looks up, looks deep into the eyes of his S...the Defender...and says, "With what authority do you speak on behalf of the defendant?"

The gentle, strong man, without hesitation, looks deep into your eyes, and then looks to his Fa...the Judge and says, "My Daddy has granted me this authority."

The Judge then gives his ruling on the objection: "Objection over-ruled. I recognize his authority to speak on behalf of the defendant."

The Accuser then menacingly rises. You can almost see tendrils of blackness emanating from him as he stands to point his finger accusingly at you. "This Man that You see before You today, Your Honor, has sinned against others. And he has taken you for granted in his life. He has denied you. He has even mocked you. He has walked away from you even when he needed you most. In the face of opposition, he has given into fear instead of trusting in you. He has worshiped false gods and taken your name in vain. Now let's look at his walk of faith. It's pathetic. It's filled with apathy. How can he even claim to have been a witness for you, your Honor? He only acknowledged you when others did the same. He only praised you when it wouldn't embarrass him. He only prayed when he was in a crisis. I, Satan the Accuser, stand before you today, your Honor, to ask for this man's life. I ask you to give the only just verdict there is: eternal damnation in the fires of Hell. The prosecution rests, Your Honor."

The air hangs heavy with guilt, punishment, and shame. You sit there wondering what the Judge must think of you. With downcast eyes, you try to meet the eyes of your Defender. You can't. Your eyes are filling with tears of shame as you sit there. You know the charges to be true. You are guilty of everything that was said.

As if your Defender can read your thoughts, you feel his hand on your shoulder. He gives a gentle, reassuring squeeze. You lift your face to meet his eyes, expecting condemnation, and yet finding none. Instead, you see only gentle Grace, tender Mercy. A sigh escapes your lips as you begin to feel a sense of assurance. Maybe all is not lost. *There is Hope.*

Your Defender introduces himself to you finally. He says in a whisper, "My name is Jesus. You know Me. You have walked with Me and I with you. You have called on My name. When you look to the Accuser, you lose your Hope. When you look to Me, your Hope is restored. Satan would like this Court to forget two important facts here today."

The Judge turns to the Defender and says, "The Defense may state their case."

Jesus stands, looks to the bench, and says, "Daddy, I thank you for hearing our case today." Satan looks surprised at that. "Daddy, before you stands a Man who was preyed upon by temptation. Out of his woundedness, he made choices...ones that weren't good. And the very Accuser that stands before you in condemnation of this Man is also the one who provided the bait for every trap to which this Man fell prey. Daddy, since the Garden, you know the sly wiles of Satan. You know how he beguiles his subjects into believing his lies. Satan, the Accuser, would like this Court to forget two important facts here today: first, he would like us to forget that restitution has already been made for all of eternity, for all sins ever to be committed by my death on the cross and by my resurrection, because of Love...out of which comes Mercy and Grace.

"And second, he would like us to forget that anyone who calls on my name will be saved from death and eternal damnation. And your Honor, if you would check the record, the Book of Life, I believe you will find the name of the defendant clearly written there in my handwriting. Your Honor, I ask for the life of this Man to be spared."

The Judge pulls out a large tome filled with pages upon pages of names. He scans the pages until he comes upon your name. You notice that as he flips through the pages, that there are many empty pages yet to be filled. Whose names will be written there, you wonder? The moment passes. Your thoughts turn back towards your judgment. For a brief moment, you are tempted to glance at your Accuser. Instead, with confidence, you turn to look into the loving eyes of your Defender, Jesus. With that one look, you have all the confidence of Heaven. Because in those eyes you see Love incarnate.

The Judge then asks you to rise. He looks at you with penetrating eyes. You can feel his eyes searching the furthest recesses of your heart. And there, in the depths of your heart, he finds that his son has made his home. He sees the wounds of your life...the ones that provided you bad information out of which you made horrible choices that only caused you and others more pain. And you sense that he is ready to pronounce his judgment. "Regarding the charges of being guilty of sin and of being lukewarm in the faith, this Court finds the Defendant..."

The air is heavy.

"...guilty."

His words echo through your mind. That one word, *guilty*, carries with it the weight of eternity.

With that, the Accuser shouts with triumph. He has won. You are defeated. You know the fate which awaits you. You notice a look passing between the Judge and the Defender...the Father and the Son. It's a knowing look. There are tears of pain and yet great Joy in that look. The Defender looks at you reassuringly. The Judge looks at you with great Mercy and Joy as He says, "*But*...the price of restitution for these sins has already been paid." And with that, you see the deep abiding scars in the wrists and ankles of your Savior, for that is what he is: Savior...and Friend...not simply Jesus the Defender...but also Jesus the Savior...Jesus the Friend.

The gavel is again slammed down three times, echoing your three denials, reminding you again of Grace. With tears of unspeakable joy, you fall to your knees before the Daddy and his Son. And you realize in that moment that they are One, and that you are greatly loved.

Thomas a Kempis wrote: "If today thou art not prepared, how wilt thou be so tomorrow? Tomorrow is uncertain, and how knowest thou that thou shalt live till tomorrow? When it is morning, think that thou mayest die before night; and when evening comes, dare not to promise thyself the next morning. Be thou therefore always in readiness, and so lead thy life that death may never take thee unprepared."

If you died today, what would the ruling be in the decision in the case of: The Accuser versus _____. (fill in your name)?

Who is your defending attorney? What is his reputation? Is it anyone other than Jesus? If so, you need a new attorney. Trust me on this one...no, better yet...trust *him*. Call out the name of Jesus today. Ask him to be your Defender. Ask him to make his home in your heart. Trust him to be your Savior. You don't need another person to mediate between you and God.

You are guilty. So am I. However, if you call on the name of Jesus, there will be extenuating circumstances when it comes time for your trial. And your case will be dismissed.

You are Loved.

SHADOW DANCING

COLOSSIANS 2:8-9

Once upon a time, a young boy went for a walk with his father. When they had reached a nice copse of trees, the father suggested they play a game of hide-and-go-seek. The boy readily accepted. He loved to spend time with his father. He loved the wonderful surprise of hiding and being found. He loved the wonderful fear he felt every time he had to find his father. The boy hid first. The father began to count...1...2...3...the boy ran off to hide. He found a great place to hide behind a large fallen tree. He even covered himself up with some sticks and leaves to hide even better. He thought he had the best hiding place ever.

And then he heard his father yell, "Ready or not, here I come." He could hear his father walking through the woods, looking high and low. And then he heard footsteps come closer and closer and closer until... "Ollie, ollie oxen free! There you are!" And the father reached right down with great assurance and confidently pulled the boy from his hiding place.

"That was a pretty good hiding place, son." the father said.

"Dad, how did you find me so fast? I had such a great hiding place!"

"Son, that was easy. I know you so well. I know how you think. I know how you smell, how you breathe, how you walk. I know when you get up in the morning and when you go to bed at night. I know the hair on your head. And I know how you like to hide. Because I know you so well, I was able to find you so easily."

"Okay, Dad. Now it's your turn to hide!" And so the boy buried his face into his arms and began to count while his daddy ran off to hide. The boy decided to cheat a little bit. He counted really, really fast and didn't yell, but only spoke in a normal voice, "Ready or not, here I come." He hoped that he could catch his father not having found a hiding place yet.

And so he did. As he rounded a corner, he saw his daddy's shadow just disappearing. The boy ran on after the shadow. And as he began to catch up to the shadow, he saw it go behind a tree. Now he knew he had his daddy! He crept up to the tree. His heart was beating wildly in his chest, threatening to leap right out. He knew how his father loved to jump out and surprise him when found. And so with fear wrapped in awe, he crept closer and closer to the tree. He checked his breathing, controlled it. He didn't even rustle any of the leaves as he walked. The tree was now directly in front of him. All he had to do was to peek around the tree and his father would be found! He took a slow, deep breath, and said, "Gotcha..."

His daddy wasn't there. How could that be? He followed his father's shadow right up to this very tree. The boy was perplexed.

There was another tree just a few feet away. It was a large tree...large enough for a grown man to easily hide behind. The boy sat down at its base to try to figure out this puzzle. And as if his thoughts were heard by his daddy, he felt a hand on his shoulder and heard his father's voice.

"Son, you only chased after my shadow. You never sought me directly. Shadows will go away when they are cut off from their Source of Light. But I will never go away, because I am the Source of Light. When you want to find me, don't go after my shadow, look directly for me."

Have you ever played with your shadow? From where you are right now, can you make a shadow? Or, maybe on your lunch break, step outside for a couple of minutes and look for your shadow today. I want you to notice some things about your shadow:

- It moves with you.
- It mirrors you.
- It becomes distorted depending upon where you move in relationship to the source of light
- It doesn't always exist
- It is a representation of yourself...your shadow is not you

Your shadow moves with you. Where you go, it goes. It mirrors your every movement. But, only as well as it is able depending upon where you stand in relationship to the source of light. If the source of light is directly perpendicular to the surface upon which your shadow is cast, the mirroring of your movements is nearly perfect. However, change the angle only slightly and the distortion of your shadow becomes readily apparent. Another thing about your shadow...take away the source of light and you take away your shadow. Shadows don't always exist. And, your shadow only represents you. It's a facsimile. It's only an image...it's not tangible.

At all times, we are supposed to seek God. Instead, so many people only seek his shadow. They only seek a transitory image of God and not God's self. If you have experienced loss and seek comfort from a friend who knows God, you will only find the shadow of God...maybe not even that. Because if your friend happens to be having a weak time in their faith, you may not find even the shadow of God, because they themselves have turned away from the Source of Light in their lives. If you are in pain and you seek your only comfort in medication, again, you will find only the shadow of God. Medicine is a gift from God, to be sure, but it is still only a part of God's shadow. If you are lonely and you seek fulfillment in the arms of another person, you will find only a shadow of the fulfillment that you will receive from being in the arms of God.

Shadows are finicky and wily. They're hard to catch because they are so often distorted. Our woundedness distorts our vision. And thus, we so often only seek shadows of Grace, Love, and Mercy...rather than the True Source of these.

But that is the nature of shadows...it's not the nature of God. God wants us to come to him. God desires it. God wants to be found. And when we find God, the Scripture tells us that "fullness comes together for you." God may use his shadow to offer some comfort, some easing of pain, some fulfillment to our loneliness. But ultimately, all shadows fade with the disappearance of their Light Source. And when we seek a shadow, we often come up empty-handed.

Today, imagine that your life is like walking in the woods, playing a game of hide-and-go-seek with your Daddy in Heaven. When it is your turn to hide, you are so easily found because God knows you so well. From what are you hiding?

But when God hides, we so often only seek a shadow of God. And so God says to you today: "My child, you only chased after my shadow. You never sought me directly. Shadows will go away when they are cut off from their

Source of Light. But I will never go away, because I AM the Source of Light...the Source of Love. When you want to find me, don't go after my shadow, look directly for me. If you seek my shadow, you will find the emptiness of the universe. Instead, seek my face. Come to me and you will find the fullness that comes together for you, through me. Stop dancing with my shadow and dance with me, my dear one."

"Ollie-ollie-oxen-free!"

THE BEIGE GOSPEL

1 TIMOTHY 4:1-2

I love purple days. When I'm having a purple day, I'm trusting in God for every outcome in every moment. I see Joy present in every moment, because I know that God is my strength, and God's strength is my joy. Purple is passionate. Purple blazes forth with color. Purple isn't non-committal. Purple is the opposite of beige in my color palette.

I hate beige days. When I'm having a beige day, I'm having a difficult time sensing God's presence and will in my life. It's difficult to sense Joy, because I'm trusting in my strength and not God's. My strength causes me to grit my teeth...to grin and bear it. Beige is just so...blah. It's beige for crying out loud! Beige does not stand out...it defines suburbia. Beige defines what it means to be non-committal. Beige is bland.

And so often, we downplay Good News and make it OK News...Nice News...and consequently, we color it beige.

We have this tremendous capacity to downplay things. Do you know what a euphemism is? Euphemisms are usually used to downplay, or disguise the real depth of meaning. For instance, instead of saying "He died," we say "He kicked the bucket," "He passed away," "He's in a better place now," and on and on. I'm sure you could come up with a few of these if you tried. So often we use euphemisms to downplay what is actually happening.

And after a while of using the euphemism, we begin to believe that things might not be all that bad. We begin to believe in our own falsehoods. See, there I go...a euphemism: falsehood...let's call it what it is...a lie. Let's do away with these words: fib, little white lie, falsehood, prevarication, misrepresentation, tale, and fabrication.

Fibs are not cute. Little white lies do not help anyone. A falsehood is the opposite of the truth. Prevarications are premeditated lies. Misrepresentations hide the truth. Tales grow taller and further from the truth. And a fabrication is something you make up...it isn't real.

It's time we start gettin' honest around here. It's time we stopped worrying about offending people and being "nice." Please show me where in the Bible it tells us to be "nice" to each other. I see that we're supposed to be gentle and compassionate. But I don't see where Jesus tells us to be nice.

Was Jesus being nice when he said, "I didn't come to bring peace, but a sword?" Was Jesus being nice when he told people that if they were a stumbling block to someone in the faith, that it would be better for them to have a millstone tied around their neck and be cast into the sea? Was Jesus being nice when he angrily walked into the Temple, chasing people out, turning over their tables?

Nothing beige here.

The Gospel is offensive, my friends. And when we try to soften it...to euphemize it...it loses its power. It falls on deaf ears. It's beige.

Imagine some of these famous quotations from Jesus, re-colored beige:

"You have heard that it was said, 'Do not commit adultery.' But I tell you that anyone who looks at a

woman lustfully is not that bad of a person. Lustful thoughts are no big whoop." Matthew 5:27,28

"Jesus said to her, 'I am the resuscitation attempt and the crossed fingers. He who believes in me might live, even though he dies...that is, if we can resuscitate them...and whoever lives and believes in me is pretty lucky.'" John 11:25, 26

"This may be to my father's glory, that you bear a little fruit, showing yourselves to be nice people." John 15:8

"If you continue reading my stories, you are sort of my acquaintances; and you will know some good stories, and the stories will be a good way to relax." John 8:31,32

Now, the Purple Gospel (as it should be)

"You have heard that it was said, 'Do not commit adultery.' But I tell you that anyone who looks at a woman lustfully has already committed adultery with her in his heart." Matthew 5:27,28

"Jesus said to her, 'I am the resurrection and the life. He who believes in me will live, even though he dies; and whoever lives and believes in me will never die.'" John 11:25, 26

"This is to my father's glory, that you bear much fruit, showing yourselves to be my disciples." John 15:8

"If you continue in my word, you are truly my disciples; and you will know the truth, and the truth will set you free." John 8:31,32

Yuck! A Beige Gospel is to a Minnesota Tuna Hot Dish as the Purple Gospel is to Cajun Chicken Gumbo. It becomes the Gospel of the least common denominator... appealing to many, yet effective to none.

When we recolor anything in our lives to be beige, we hide the real truth of the matter. We lie.

When we soften the Gospel...when we recolor it beige...when we de-offensify it...we in fact, lie. Let's call it what it is. A Beige Gospel is a lie.

I praise God today that the Gospel...the Good News...*God's Love* is not beige...by any stretch of the imagination. For if it were, we would not be saved from our sins, and Hell would be our future. We need to move past the idea of not offending. Jesus offended people wherever he went. And he did this, because he wanted to reach the least, the last, and the lost because in his eyes, they are the Most, the First, and the Found! When we preach a Beige Gospel, we in effect tell God that we don't care about reaching the least, the last, and the lost...and I think, we break his heart.

The Scripture for our devotion tells of those who are liars...who have lost their capacity for the truth because they have lied for so long. I see these people in our churches today. They have softened the Gospel so much, they've watered it down...they've colored it beige...and it hits about as hard as a Nerf ball. They have come to believe in their lies. They believe their Beige Gospel is offensive. John Wesley said that he knew he had been faithful to preaching the Gospel if someone told him they were offended. I wonder how often these people are told that they have offended someone?

Preach a Purple Gospel today! Be offensive...especially to "religious" people. Jesus offended them wherever he went, and look at the people he reached: folks just like you and me. Of course, in the end it got him nailed to a cross...but that's another story...an offensive one...a true one.

THE GREAT BUBBLE BLOB

1 CORINTHIANS 5:6-8

I had a friend in high school, for whom I often house-sat. Admittedly, my motivations for house-sitting were not entirely altruistic. How often does a seventeen- or eighteen-year-old guy get a house to himself for a week? On these occasions, whilst my friends were on vacation, I was at their house with a stack of videos (tons of "redemptive" violence, of course), bags of chips, cans of pop, and large pizzas and double-cheeseburgers all to myself. During their vacations, I would go on a marathon video-munchy-couch-potato-palooza.

On one of these occasions, I figured I'd better get the dishes done before they got home so I began to load the dishwasher. A bit of history for you: growing up, I never had a dishwasher. We did our dishes by hand with Palmolive, a rag, and flour-sack towels to dry them when finished. Those of you overachievers who like to work ahead are probably beginning to put the pieces together already. I got all the dishes into the dishwasher, a feat in and of itself for an inexperienced, novice dishwasher operator like me. And then I looked underneath the kitchen sink for the box of powdered dishwasher soap. I grabbed the luminescent green box and heard the pitter-patter of about five granules of soap powder. Truly not enough to do the job.

I dug underneath their sink some more, thinking there might be some left in the back of the cupboard or something. But alas and forsooth, I found nothing. Well, nothing that is, except a bottle of Palmolive. Uh huh. Are you getting it yet?

Being a child of the 70s and 80s, I remembered clearly what happened on the one episode of the *Brady Bunch* when one of the boys was washing clothes and poured in an entire box of detergent. The washing machine came to life and began spewing forth prodigious amounts of suds. I had learned my lessons well from TV (Hey, it's where I learned math, grammar, science, and history, you know! Do you remember *Schoolhouse Rock*?)

Don't put too much soap into the machine.

I also was aware of the concentrated nature of dish soap and so I figured that one drop ought to be just fine to put in the dishwasher. I turned the dishwasher on and just about then, my pizza arrived. I grabbed the pizza, popped in a movie, and sat down on the couch in my gluttonous reverie.

After about a half hour, I began to see movement out of the corner of my eye. At first, I ignored it, figuring I was just imagining things. After a few more minutes, I knew I was seeing something and so I turned to look...

And there, creeping around the corner, was a blob of suds, coming to get me. I yelled something profound like "Holy bubbles, Batman!" leapt from my perch on the couch and ran to the kitchen, sliding through the Great Bubble Blob. I quickly turned off the dishwasher and began to mop up the suds. And then I called for help. I called my mom.

"Mom!"

"What's wrong, Shane?" she asked, sounding concerned.

"Well, I ah...I goofed, mom." I said, kind of sheepishly.

"What happened?" she asked, being a cool mom.

"Um, it's like this...I...well...I put dish soap into the dishwasher..."

Before I could even finish she yelled, "You what?!"

"I put dish soap into the dishwasher...but I only put in one drop."

"Shane. Oh, honey." she said in her thick Minnesotan accent, "Well, I guess you learned better on that one! Here's what you need to do, empty the dishwasher and run it several times through with just cold water. That'll make the suds go away and you'll be fine."

"Thanks, Mom." I said.

"You're welcome. Good luck," she said.

Well, she was right. A couple of hours later, I had the mess all cleaned up. And when my friends returned home, they were none the wiser. But I told them anyway. I think I said something brilliant like, "Did you know you can get soap suds to shrink with cold water?"

If you put in the wrong soap, life can go seriously awry.

That's pretty much what Paul, the first century church starter, was telling us in the fifth chapter of his first letter to the church in Corinth. "Hey folks, ya know what? If you keep pumping yourselves up, you're headed for a fall. Yes, it feels good to be loved by God. Yes, it's wonderful that we are created in God's image. It feels good to be noticed and recognized, doesn't it? But guess what? It ain't all about you. It's about God...it's about LOVE. So, stop puttin' in that stuff that's going to puff you up and make you appear larger or better than you are. And start only putting in what will make you to be the kind of person God has created you to be."

For me, it's sometimes just a matter of putting on some clothes, cologne, and a little extra gel in the hair and I'm puffing myself up to look better than I really am. Other times I'll exaggerate a story to make it look better. I get to thinking things like, "If only I drove a brand-new, emerald-green, 1969 Camaro, then I'd be cool. Or if I only bought my entire wardrobe from whatever name-brand stores are popular, then I'd be all right. If only I ate at the right restaurants. If only I had enough money. If only I had a cool boat. If only I wore the right shoes. If only I had the right friends. If only...if only..."

And then God gently says, "If only you'd turn to *me*, dear one."

"What? Who's that?" I ask.

"You know Who I Am! *Hello!* Don't you remember calling out to me when that car almost smashed into you? If only you'd turn to me...if only you'd put me in your life first, then everything else will fall into place as it should be. You won't need to build yourself up at all if you put me in first...if you put *Love* in first. Because I will build you up in a way which will astonish and amaze everyone. I will build you up to be the person you are created to be. So, what's it going to be? Are you going to continue to put in all that other stuff so that you can feel better about yourself? Or are you going to turn to me?"

"Can I buy a vowel?" I ask.

God laughs and says, "Sure, you can buy an I."

"An I?" I ask.

"Yes," says God. "I Am."

"You are. *You* are. You *are*. YOU ARE!!!"

God turns to the Archangel Michael and says, "Hey, Mikey! I think he likes it!"

"I think I get it now God. It ain't all about me...it's all about you...it's all about your Love."

"Ah, young grasshopper, now you're beginning to see," says God.

"God?"

"Yes, Shane."

"You get to be first in my life."

"About time." says God with a smile.

FISH STORIES

MATTHEW 4:19

It was early when God woke me up. My eyes were heavy with flakes of sleep still on my lashes. I gazed into the mirror and saw a disheveled, tired man with unkempt hair before my eyes and after a brief moment, realized I was looking upon myself. Have you ever had that feeling of wondering about the identity of the person in the mirror? I guess in some ways I was relieved it was me. I mean to wake and find someone staring back at you in the mirror, that means it's going to be a good day, right? And if the mirror fogs up, that's a bonus!

And yet there was a note of dissatisfaction hanging dissonantly upon the stale cabin air. Psalm 139 tells us we're "fearfully and wonderfully made." And what I wondered at that grim hour was this: am I living this way? Am I living as if I was fearfully and wonderfully made by God?

Am I living as a wonderful, hand-crafted, unique work of Love created by God? Am I living up to my full potential?

Awfully deep thoughts to have without the aid of coffee that early in the morning. I stepped to the front door of the cabin and looked upon the misty surface of the lake. I opened the door a crack to test the temperature and realized with a small shudder that it was still a bit cold and it was continuing to lightly rain. I put on a couple of long sleeved shirts, my baseball cap, and a borrowed jacket and stepped forth with purpose. I was feeling called to fish.

Captain Ahab I'm not. For those who know me, they'll tell you I'm not a professional angler. So, if you're wanting to catch whatever legendary creature happens to dwell in your lake, I'm probably not the guy to call. And yet this morning, I was having this strong urge to fish. It was miserable outside. It was about forty-five degrees, rainy, and the sun was nowhere to be found. Why would I want to fish on a morning like this? For the life of me, I couldn't figure out a good reason. There were perfectly good blankets and a pot of coffee awaiting back inside the cabin. But I could not resist the urge.

I started on the dock. After about a half hour, I had caught a couple of rock bass which, I'm told, are to be thrown back. And so I did. About an hour into the morning, I decided to start up a boat and take it for a spin out to a weed bed. Forty-five degrees with wind and rain, magnified by the speed of the boat felt a bit like Antarctica to me and as I reached my destination, shivering and very wet, I questioned my wisdom as I'm sure you may question my sanity. I tried this until it started to rain a lot harder and decided to head back. Of course, about the time I got back, the rain let up a bit and I thought of going back out, but I was just too cold.

And yet, I knew I couldn't give up. For some reason, I felt a strong urge to continue casting my line in and out of what seemed like God-forsaken water to me that morning. And after a while, it began to pay off. Not only was I regularly getting bites at the end of my line, but I was beginning to reel some in as well. I caught several more rock bass, a few sunfish, and two northern pike, 17 and 20 inches respectively. I must have cast my line into that lake several hundred times over the several hours I was out that morning, and for what? A few measly fish, some of which I had to throw back?

Several hundred tries to catch a couple of fish worth keeping.

In the midst of the cold and the rain, the Lord began to speak to me about fishing. God reminded me of a few things:

1) First of all, I need to start where I am. I don't need to begin by traveling to some far off land to fish for people. There are plenty waiting to be caught by the Good News of God's Love right here at the end of our own docks. These are people we walk by every day and barely nod our heads too, let alone share Love with them. Let me ask you this, if you had a campfire going in your yard and some neighbor you hardly knew, or better yet, the evil neighbor you can't stand were blindly walking towards your campfire, about to step into the flames and get burned, wouldn't you do everything in your power to warn them? And that's just the heat from a campfire!

The fires of Hell would be much worse and of course, last forever. So why aren't we telling our neighbors? Our family members? Those at the corner store? Our coworkers? Why? I think the answer is simple: we're afraid and uncomfortable. We're afraid our fishing attempts will be rejected and we'll be ridiculed. Why are we so afraid to tell people that they can heal from the wounds of their earlier lives? Why are we so afraid to share with people that we make horrible decisions that we call "sin" out of that woundedness...and that a Loving God only wants us to heal so that we can be forgiven?

2) Fishing requires persistence. I had to go out for several hours in adverse circumstances just to catch a few worth keeping. It's the same in our fishing for people. We will have to do this all the time, everywhere we go, casting Love over and over again just to find a few ears ready to hear the message and be caught by Good News.

3) It doesn't matter where I cast my line. What matters is that I'm casting and not just standing there. God calls us to cast Love all around us wherever we go and not to care about who listens and who does not.

4) I don't get to choose who I catch. It's not up to me to pick and choose. In fact, in fishing, I'm not down at the bottom of the lake, guiding and directing which fish to bite my line. I can do my best to make the conditions better by using different lures and hooks. When I fish for people, I can "be all things to all people so that I might save some." I can use the native language spoken by different groups and go to where they are. But in the end, the Message is still the same: we are sinners needing to repent...we are wounded people who need to heal, and we need a savior from our sin and his name is Jesus. In spite of my best efforts, it is up to God to move in peoples' hearts and bring them to a place of being receptive to Love. I don't get to choose who will hear and who will ignore. That's not up to me. But casting my line, the Love of God, is up to me.

Friends, people all around us at this very moment are dying and living in Hell. What are we doing about it? Just living a good life and hoping they'll notice? What if they don't? When Jesus stopped by Andrew and Simon's nets that day and asked them to drop what they were doing, literally leaving behind their way of life for several years of front-line ministry, telling people that the Kingdom of God is here and they must repent and begin to follow the narrow path which leads to life, he was calling them far beyond what was comfortable. He was calling them from their homes, their families—their entire way of life.

We get discouraged and are afraid to share the Love of God with even those whom we Love, let alone complete strangers as Jesus and the disciples did.

We have the same power and the same God, friends. Of what should we be afraid? A little rejection in the face of eternal consequences? It seems we do not trust God's Love very much to do its work.

Captain Ahab I'm not when it comes to fishing for fish. But I'm certainly working on a promotion when it comes to fishing for people. How about you?

THE MESSAGE

GALATIANS 1:6-9

Once upon a time in a land not so far from here, there was a city which lived in confusion. The city, Christiana by name, founded itself upon some Basic Precepts and Principles, all of which came from the mouth of the Namesake of their city. In fact, the people of Christiana were so proud of their Namesake and of his Basic Precepts and Principles, that they would go off in teams to neighboring towns and villages to tell people about their Namesake and the things he taught.

And so it happened that the neighboring towns and villages began also to live by the Basic Precepts and Principles as taught by the Namesake of Christiana. At least, they were giving it their best shot. And the Message of the Namesake of Christiana began to spread far and wide. In fact, it came to reach every shore of every nation. The Message of the Namesake of Christiana, his Basic Precepts and Principles by which to live, came to the point of being the predominant teaching in the world. It seemed that the Message would one day live in each person's heart everywhere.

Until one day...

One day there came a man to one of the neighboring villages of Christiana. He called himself the Beguiler, and he was so beguiling that nobody realized that his name meant Deceiver. The Beguiler was slick and sly and slithered through the city speaking subtle deceptions. Nothing he said wasn't true...it just wasn't *the* Truth.

Everywhere he went, he spoke these different truths and the townspeople would look at him, thinking there must be something wrong with what he said. But they just couldn't put their fingers on it. They would look at him with their heads cocked to the side, brows furrowed, brains churning away trying to figure out what was different. They would think for a few moments, and then shrug their shoulders and walk away, basically accepting what was said. Instead of one Truth residing in their hearts now many began to take up residence there.

It was taught that the only way to make it to the City of Gold which the Namesake spoke of, was to follow the Namesake of Christiana, to believe his Basic Precepts and Principles. It was a very basic Message. But the Beguiler, having spoken deceptively so often, realized that the foundation for his "message" had been laid. And so one day, he rang the town bell so everyone would gather in the town square. Once gathered, the Beguiler smiled his most disarming smile. As he did, hearts melted. He was a handsome one and smooth too. Even the men elbowed each other and said things like, "He's quite a guy," or "What a stud!"

The Beguiler then began to speak: "My friends...you are my friends, right?" Crowd applauds wildly. The Beguiler put his hands up to signal the crowd to quiet so they would listen. "My friends, I've asked you here today so that I could reveal the "truth" to you all. Because you see, my friends, I care about you all, but in a much different way than the Namesake of Christiana. I care about you here and now and not just in the pie in the sky City of Gold. I care about what happens to each one of you today. In fact, I care so much that I promise to fulfill your dreams, your wants, your desires...everything you gave up for the Namesake, I promise to give back to you today. Do you want your lives back?" Again, wild applause from the gathered crowd. "Then claim it dear friends, reclaim your independence...reclaim your dignity and pride...reclaim the pursuit of things after which you lust and strive. Today is a day of Independence. Today, I proclaim this small town and each one of you my messengers to carry a truth to this world, namely that they do not have to bend their knee or confess with their mouths the Message as taught by that other guy...what was his name again? It escapes me. No longer do you have to surrender your will. No longer do you have to give up your wants. No longer do you have to sacrifice here and now. *No longer!*"

And with that last proclamation...which by the way...is true...it's just not *the* Truth...the crowd went nuts. They started to rock cars back and forth. People were shouting and whooping and hollering. Someone set off some firecrackers. A policeman thought it was a gun and he pulled his gun and took aim and shot into the crowd. And thus began a riot which continues still today. It's not always so brash and crazy. But the riot goes on and on. And it goes on, seeping its way from village to village, town to town. Sometimes the riot is a whisper in the ear of a child saying "You don't have to do that." Other times the riot is a melee breaking loose in the heart of a city which had been claimed for the Namesake. Lives are lost...both metaphorically and in reality.

And the riot continues because of *a* message which is not *the* Message.

Somewhere outside time and space, the Namesake mourns over his villages and towns. He mourns those who accept the other message proclaimed by the Beguiler. He weeps. He weeps for those who sacrifice his promises for the empty ones of the Beguiler. He weeps for those who are deceived. He weeps for those who give up and give in and eventually give out.

But in the next moment, the Namesake stands to his feet wiping the tears away, for even though he watches his friends getting deceived, he knows the Ultimate Victory is already won. And in moments like these, the Hope in the Message which he came to share washes over him and instead of weeping, He dances.

He dances for you.

He dances for me.

He dances so the lost may see.

THE CASTLE OF GOD

1 JOHN 5:18-20

Being a Christian ain't easy.

This just MAY be the understatement of all time. When I first became a Christian, I thought: "Hey! Now my life is going to be great! Everything will be perfect. No worries. And you know that problem I had with those sins I was committing? Done! I'll never sin again."

Ahem.

Well, I must admit, I have sinned a few times since then. (This may qualify for the second greatest understatement) My life has not been perfect, in fact, there have been horrendous struggles and challenges. At times, I HAVE worried. My life as a Christian was not shiny-happy-yellow-smiley-smooth-sailin'. There have been moments of shiny-happy. Glimpses of yellow-smiley. Stretches of smooth sailin'.

What I neglected to realize, is that I was under attack...and that the attacks do not stop when you've become a Christian. Indeed, the attacks seem to get worse.

Imagine that you are in a castle. The walls of your castle are the defenses you must maintain to prevent the attacks from getting through. Now, there's no way for you to stop the attacks from coming, because you're in the castle. But there are ways for you to strengthen your defenses and even occasionally go on the offense. By participating daily in the Spiritual Disciplines (those things we intentionally do to live lives that reflect God's Love...the things we do to Love God and Love those around us) you maintain and even strengthen your defenses. In fact, over time, your walls around your castle will grow stronger, taller, and thicker. You must also realize that you have God's power to rely on in this one. God's angels are a part of your defense. They walk the walls with you looking for enemies scaling your defenses. They ride out in sorties to attack the Enemy's forces, thus, weakening their attacks on you. The power that is in the Love of God flows through the walls of your castle, giving it all the strength it needs. Being a Christian is like being the king of the castle in so many ways. You must know your force's strengths and weaknesses. You must do whatever it takes to maintain your defenses.

The enemy will use the tiniest crack in the wall of your castle, and exploit it against you. Your wall must remain intact, and smooth...because if the enemy can even get one finger into a crack, then your defenses have been breached.

What dismays me is when I see churches neglecting to tell their people that they must build castles. They never tell that life will still contain challenges and obstacles. They never share the fact that the attacks on their exist-ence will not only *not cease*, but may even continue in greater intensity.

There are churches on one side of the fence who believe in the power of God's Love and who know that the enemy is real and alive who tell their people that life will be prosperous and perfect once they become a Christian. They neglect to share the need for the defense of a castle.

And there are churches on the other side of the fence who do not believe in the evil power of the enemy and his evil angels. They neglect to share the need for the defense of a castle.

So, my dear friends, I'm telling you today: your life as a Christian will not be without attack. And there is a fallen angel out there named Satan who wants to destroy that which God is building within your heart.

You need the protection and defense of a castle.

Have you reaffirmed your faith lately? Have you said his name right out loud: Jesus! I love you so much. I want you to be the Leader of my life. I confess that I have sinned against you and your children and I ask for your forgiveness today. Cleanse my heart, my life of all that does not honor you. Help me to be the person you created me to be...the best version of myself. Please build your castle around my life. I do not want to continue in a life of sin. I no longer want to live out of my wounds, but out of your Love.

If you are able to pray something like this, the main part of your castle has been constructed. You have placed your faith in Jesus. But to maintain it...to build the walls of your castle even stronger and higher, you need to daily practice Spiritual Discipline. You need to regularly confess your sins and ask for forgiveness. You need to fast and give of yourself and your finances so that you rely only on the power of God in your life...rather than rely on yourself.

My friends, lest I be misunderstood: the Spiritual Disciplines do not save you. Only the Grace of God can do that. But the Spiritual Disciplines gain you protection from the evil wiles and attacks of the enemy, who will try to wheedle his way into your life, exploiting the tiniest of cracks to infiltrate the pure heart of Love that God is creating within you.

Take an inventory of your castle today. How are your defenses? Where are the cracks in the walls of your castle? What are the sins you are still committing? From what wounds do you still need to heal? For it is out of our woundedness that we sin...that we live lives that are not Loving. As you stand atop the wall of your castle, notice the battle being waged around you for your soul. The sounds of battle are so very close and seem so dangerous when the walls of your castle have not been sufficiently maintained through a close walk with Jesus. Turn your face to the skies...feel the rays of the Love of God upon your face. Feel his Love for you and feel the strength it provides. And now notice, that the more you bask in his love—the more you delight in the presence of God, the stronger and higher the walls of your castle become, and the more distant the sounds of battle seem.

Hmmmm. Imagine that.

THE LION IS AT YOUR SIDE

REVELATION 5:5

There he stands. He is terrible, fierce, powerful, and mighty. His head is held straight and tall, His mane a crown of golden glory. He is lithe, his muscles taut and toned. His claws gleam like swords. He is King, of that, there can be no question. For Who could stand like that and not be?

He is regal without effort, his royalty evident in his mighty roar. His tail, swishes back and forth with patient agitation. The source of which is you. Does this surprise you? Who are you that you could cause such a feeling in such as this? Who are you, O Son of Adam? Who are you, Daughter of Eve, to cause such consternation in the King?

Who am I?

Yes, who am I to cause agitation in this King? And why do I cause it? Is it my very presence? He—the King—looks at me as I think the question. If I didn't know better, I would swear I saw him smile. And the King shakes his mighty head, his glorious mane swishing back and forth with his answer. If it is not my presence that bothers him, then what? The clothes I wear? The music to which I listen...the images at which I look? The friends with whom I associate? The words which issue forth from my mouth? What is it?

The King looks at me intently. Those eyes...those deep, azure eyes bore into my thoughts, searching for the answer. As he looks, he raises his chin slightly. The word dignity comes to mind when I look at him. But this word is not my answer. He knows I know. And I think I do, but I do not want to say. For to utter it, would make it so.

I ask if it is my clothes, my music, my friends, my speech. The King, this Lion of Judah, nods once, and then cocks his head to one side, as if he's saying, "And?" His tail is still twitching. I can see that he is still agitated.

Ah, but remember, the agitation is patient. I realize he is agitated *for* me, not *with* me. And that is why he is also patient. He wants me to know what he knows. He wants me to *know*...

Realization dawns upon my consciousness. And I am ashamed. Yes, my clothes bother him when they proclaim Self...when they proclaim Pride. He is agitated for he wants to clothe me with Righteousness, for Righteousness' sake.

My music is a source of irritation when it proclaims the false glory of this world and denies the Glory of the kingdom which God has prepared for us. The images I view are idols which can never equal God's Love. Yes, he—our King—this Lion of Judah has prepared a Kingdom for you and for me. Those mighty talons have carved a mansion in a City of Gold with special places—places of royalty, for we are his heirs. Did you know that? Son of Adam, Daughter of Eve, you are Princes and Princesses in the Kingdom? Do you walk that way? Do you talk that way? Do you carry yourself regally or as one condemned? As his heirs, the music to which we listen should warrant his ear...the images we view, his eyes. Are these things worthy of God's attention? Often...yes. Sometimes, and sadly, no.

I realize also, that it is not the friends with whom I associate that bother him. Rather, it is the fact that I fall into their patterns of behavior, abdicating my royal inheritance. My King asks simply that I be a Prince in his Kingdom so that others will hearken to his call. So very often, I act like a vagabond peasant beggar in the Kingdom, scraping the scraps from the garbage heap when I could be a Prince, dining at the Royal Banquet table.

My words also cause this irritation in my King. The words give false directions to those around me. So often, they give directions to the enemy's realm, and not the Kingdom of Heaven. How often have I been responsible for mis-guiding others? How often have my words pointed them in the wrong direction.

More and more, I understand the agitation of my King. The cause is simply this: He is my King whether or not I acknowledge it...and more often than not, I do not.

I fail to acknowledge God's royalty, thus abdicating my own.

Our King wants only to walk at our side. Wherever we go, he goes. This is what he desires. And so often, we turn away. It is not our King who forsakes us. Rather, we forsake our King. We turn our backs on Love.

Would we act differently if we knew the Lion of Judah, the King of Heaven and Earth walked at our side? How would we approach a situation if we knew there was a Lion at our side? Would there be any room for fear? No way. I refuse to believe it possible. If we were to face an intimidating situation with the knowledge that our King, the Lion of Judah, with those fierce eyes and mighty talon-tipped paws walked by our side, I dare believe we would be smiling!

The Lion of Judah has triumphed! Our King is victorious and we are heirs to his victory and to his Kingdom. Daughter of Eve, you are a Princess in his Kingdom. Wear your crown knowing your King walks at your side. Son of Adam, you are a Prince in the Kingdom of Heaven, stand tall and walk with the royalty that is inherent in the crown you wear.

Fear not, dear friends, there is a Lion at your side. You are Loved.

Now live like it.

Love Overalls

Colossians 3:12-14

Once upon a time, a man went shopping for some new clothes. He went to a large mall with many clothing stores to choose from. There were many choices to be made: shirts, shoes, pants, belts, socks, and so on.

On this particular shopping trip, the man was feeling a bit full of himself, and his choices of clothing seemed to show this. He chose the nicest shirts with silk threads woven in. He only selected pants made from the finest linen. He shopped for several hours, and then went home to try on his new clothes.

He went into his bedroom and began to put on the new clothes. As soon as he was dressed, he went to look at himself in the mirror. He was amazed at himself. "Wow, what a good lookin' guy you are," he said to his reflection in the mirror.

And, to his great surprise, his reflection answered him: "Oh, you think so, eh? And what do you think of your new clothes?"

"Well, if I do say so myself, I look pretty sharp. I'm a snazzy dresser."

His reflection replied, "You think so, huh? You like your nice shirt and your fancy linen pants?"

"Well, yeah. Why, shouldn't I?" asked the man.

"Actually, you should take a closer look at the tags on your clothes. You might learn a little something about your choices of apparel."

"Okay," says the man "I'll take a look. Hmmmm...the tag on my pants says Self-Centered and the tag on my shirt says Pride. What do they mean?" asks the man.

His reflection says, "You are so blinded by yourself that you are unable to see others around you. You put on the garments of Self-Centeredness and Pride and you have only enough room in your life for yourself. I suggest that you take these items back to the store and try again."

"Really? You don't think these look good on me?"

"Absolutely not." says the reflection confidently.

{sigh} "Okay. I'll try again."

So, the man packs his new clothes back into a bag and takes them back to the store. Again he goes shopping for several hours and finds some new clothes to bring home and try on. This time, he's very anxious to see his reflection with these new clothes on.

He bought a steel grey suit, tailored to fit his body crisply. He donned the suit and then looked into the mirror.

"Mirror, mirror on the wall, who's the..." began the man.

"Okay, knock it off. We're not doin' the Snow White thing here," interrupted the reflection. "Okay, I tell you what, this isn't all that horrible, but, I've got to tell you, it's still not you."

"How can that be? The salesperson at the shop said this was "me, the whole me, and nothing but me, so help her God." said the man.

"Well, apparently she's needin' God's help." says the reflection, "because that suit just ain't you. It's Cold, Calculated, Crisp, *Unloving*."

"So, you want me to try again?" asks the man.

The reflection only nods.

The man takes off the suit, hangs it up, and returns it to the shop and begins his quest for the right clothes. He shops for many hours again, and this time, he's sure that he's got it right.

He gets home, takes the clothes out of the bag, puts them on, and then boldly and suavely steps in front of the mirror. The man looks into the mirror and shrugs, as if to say, "Well? What do you think?"

The reflection only shakes his head again. He says, "Okay, you've toned it down a bit. But, you're wearing a black shirt unbuttoned practically to your waist. Obviously, you're wearing Indifference and Lust tonight. Not good, my friend...*not good*. The black shows that again, you're thinking of yourself and not being compassionate towards the needs of others, and the whole unbuttoned thing...okay, get a life! Okay stud, I know you think you've got the "Eye of The Tiger" {sarcasm} and that you're going to be a chick-magnet with your chest showing...but, and trust me on this one, all you're showing again is how much you're thinking of yourself and not others. Can I ask you a question?"

"Okay, shoot." says the man.

"Where are you shopping for your clothes?" asks the reflection.

"Well, I've gone to the Mega Brand Name Outlet Mall Complex, of course."

"Ahhhhhh...I'm beginning to see the problem here. You're following the ways of this world. You're shopping where everybody else shops. Let me ask you another question." says the reflection.

"Go for it." says the man.

"Do you like to look like everybody else?" asks the reflection.

"No, of course not. I like to be a trend-setter."

"Well since you don't want to conform to the ways of this world, how about this, why don't you try shopping at a garage sale or a second hand store? You can find a lot of practical clothes in places like that. You'll find clothes that not a lot of people like to wear, but are way cool in God's eyes." says the reflection.

"You've got to be kidding. I wouldn't be caught dead in clothes like those." says the man.

"Well you may be caught dead in the other clothes and imagine what the neighbors will think." says the reflection. "More importantly, imagine what God will think."

"Oh. Good point."

"You know, keep your eyes open for a good pair of overalls. They're not too revealing. They're very solid, and very functional. You've got plenty of pockets to keep a healthy supply of Compassion, Kindness, and Forgiveness at hand. They're not very showy, so you'll always be Humble with a pair of overalls on. And they're not too far out, so your Self-Discipline should be in check. Now, you're not going to win any popularity contests or best-dressed man of the year awards. But, you will be well-prepared for whatever God sends your way...for whatever I send your way."

With that, the man looked in the mirror and noticed his reflection change to that of a man with Love in his eyes like he'd never seen before. He was dressed in a simple pair of overalls, and his pockets seemed to be overflowing with Compassion, Love, Forgiveness, Kindness, and Humility. There was nothing pretentious about this Man. And yet, when you looked at him, you saw a King. A King in overalls of Love.

It's true what they say, clothes really do make the man.

SIMON PETER SAYS: WAKE UP!

1 PETER 1:13-16

I have gone on several mission trips into the hills and hollers of the great state of Tennessee. Beautiful country. Rolling green hills. Morning mist meandering down the mountains. I have many memories from my times in Tennessee in mission to the wonderful residents of the areas we visited.

The conditions under which we worked were less than savory. There is almost always one hundred percent humidity down there in ninety degree heat. Your sweat doesn't evaporate to cool your skin. It just beads up and rolls down your forehead stinging your eyes with its saltiness. Your clothes are soaked by the end of the day, yet you don't feel any cooler. And you can imagine how wonderful sweaty wet jeans feel.

Furthermore, the materials and tools you are given to use are also less than savory. The tools mostly come from the deepest recesses of the purgatory of the garages of the people from whom you've borrowed them. The handles are usually frail and brittle, just waiting for too much strain upon the grain of the wood from which they're made. And of course, in the very moment you need them most, they crack under the pressure and you are left having to improvise your way out of just about every situation.

The wood you are given to build whatever you are charged with constructing is raw, rough, and untreated. Imagine a wet, jagged piece of oak. Now imagine this: you pick up a hammer; remember, the handle is old and frail and will break, you grab a rusty nail that gathered its tangerine coat simply from sitting in the humidity of this moist land, you place the nail upon the mangled wood you've been told is a two by four, and you raise your hammer to strike the nail, hopefully thrusting it into the wood, and you strike the nail.

You barely escape being called Cyclops for the rest of your life as the nail zings from the grip of your fingers and you follow through with the hammer striking the wood which by its solid nature seems much more like concrete than wood. We found that to pound nails into such wood, first you had to drill holes through which the nails could pass. One day, it took us three hours to pound eight nails.

Yes, these are the general operating conditions for mission trip work in Tennessee. Please realize that I am not exaggerating. And don't even get me started on the driving directions you are given to get to the location of your projects! Most of the projects seem nigh impossible, but you just have to go for it, rolling up your sleeves, and putting your mind into gear to solve the many problems you seem to face.

On one of our projects, we ran out of materials with which to finish our job. We called back to base camp to let them know of our situation and they said they'd send someone right out with more. Well, apparently their version of "sending someone right out" was a little different than ours. After a couple of hours had passed, and we had talked with the resident we were serving about as much as the resident wanted to be spoken with, we figured we'd take some time out to relax in the sun. We'd kick back, relax, take a load off and...

Well, you can imagine that from the hard work, the heat, and the lack of any project, many fell asleep.

Just like Peter did that night in the Garden.

When the guy from camp arrived with our supplies, we were not ready for the gift of supplies. We had grown lazy. I remember the guy who had delivered our supplies seemed less than happy with us. And to get things moving, he jumped in and began to work. He had been driving around getting supplies from different places all day long, transporting them around the county to different sites. He was just as exhausted as we...maybe more. And yet, he dove right in to work...to serve.

Because his life was shaped by God's life...energetic and blazing with holiness...with Love.

We had grown lax and lazy with complacency. We didn't search out other ways to serve the resident of the home upon which we were working. We only saw the job before us. We had fallen back into the groove of evil, being self-serving and self-centered. We began to convince ourselves that we deserved the rest...that we only signed up for the project in front of us...nothing more...but hopefully less. We saw the person as less than we and their home simply as a project.

In fact, maybe we were asleep even before we were. Maybe we were spiritually asleep. Maybe we had forsaken our Savior in sleep before we ever got into a van to travel to Tennessee.

I remember the shame I felt when I realized what the guy was doing before us: serving us...even though we stopped serving.

That must have been a lot of what Peter felt that night when he was asleep in the Garden and Jesus kept trying to wake him up. That must have been what Peter felt when the soldiers came to take Jesus away...and that's why Peter reacted with such anger and cut that man with his sword...he was angry at himself for forsaking his best friend, Jesus. And Jesus rebuked him. "Put the sword down Peter. If you live your life that way...you'll die that way."

Who better to tell us to stay awake and alert than Peter? Who better to call us out of laziness than the very one who fell asleep ten yards from the Savior of the Universe?

We are called by Peter in this passage to roll up our sleeves and put our minds into gear. He tells us to be ready for the gift that Jesus will bring when he arrives.

Do you know what it feels like to be startled from sleep? Someone is shaking you and calling your name and you jump...your heart stops for what seems like a minute...your adrenaline courses through your body to restart your failed heart...you're bewildered and feel a little crazed until you realize what is going on.

Peter is giving us a wake-up call. Hopefully, he's startling us from our sleep. Because you know what, my friends? We know better. We've been told this before. We need to stay awake and alert...always ready for the gift Jesus will bring. We may not simply do what we feel like, laying back to take a spiritual snooze when our walk of faith seems difficult or short on supplies.

"As obedient children, let yourselves be pulled into a way of life shaped by God's life, a life energetic and blazing with holiness. God said, 'I am holy; you be holy."

We are called to be holy because God is holy. We are called to be energetic and blazing with holiness because God is energetic and blazing with holiness. We are called to readiness because God is ready.

We are called to be ready for Jesus' return because he is always ready for our return.

Return to Him. Wake up. Be energetic. Blaze! And yes, be wild...Untamed today!

Stop Crying, Or I'll Give You Something To Cry About

2 Corinthians 5:9-11

Imagine being awakened at 4:00 in the morning, thrust into a brown, 1976 AMC Hornet, makers of the acclaimed Pacer, with vinyl seats that seem to emanate the very essence of the nuclear fusion which occurs in the sun, driving for hours and hours, cruising down the highway in ninety-five degree heat without air conditioning. You've got mom and dad in the front seat, and brother and sister in the back, some warm, nasty peanut-butter sandwiches on Wonder Bread that is growing a little hard around the edges, some stale grape Shasta, and a used-up book of Mad -libs. You're somewhere in the middle of Iowa and about all you can find on the radio is hog futures and Billy Dorkmeister's all-Polka, all the time station. Remember, we're in the days of AM radio. {shudder}

Now, throw in your usual brother and sister fight, and some parents who are smoking like members of the Gestapo, who've "had it up to here." And you've got a recipe for meltdown.

At this point, all it would take was one look from me to my sister. "Daaaaaaaad, he's looking at me." And of course, I'd poke her in the side for good measure and the tears would flow.

My dad had some usual responses to our shenanigans. If my sister and I would fight, or mess around, or one of us would end up crying or whining about something, my dad's usual responses were these:

---

1. "Do I have to pull this car over? Because I will. I'll pull this car over and pull your pants down in front of God and everybody." We often wondered what God and everybody would think of our butts. Sidenote: a couple of times this actually happened. I was greatly tempted to wave at people as they passed by...but I didn't think that would help my cause.

2. "Don't make me come back there, Mr., because I will!" Oh, this would be a trick Dad. Good luck driving and coming back here at the same time! Oh, and as to that "because I will" stuff, why even say this, Dad, if you weren't actually planning to do it?

3. "If you two don't stop messin' around, I'll make your butts so red you won't be able to sit down until the Tuesday of next week." This one always made us have to stop and think about how far away Tuesday was and how long our butts would be hurting. Math...it got us every time.

4. "Stop crying or I'll give you something to cry about." Here's a bright one...hey Dad, guess what, we're already crying...and it's about something!

Well, apparently whatever we were crying about wasn't something we should be crying about. But if we really needed something to cry about, Dad seemed okay with providing it.

I guess part of the point of this, is that Dad wanted us to be obedient and also wanted us to realize that things could be worse, and that whatever we were upset about, relatively speaking, wasn't all that bad. Of course, then he'd go on about the starving children in Ethiopia and I always wondered why we couldn't just send my Brussels sprouts to them.

Paul, in his second letter to the church in Corinth, is writing to a group of people who are frustrated with the way things are going and they're blaming all of it on him! Paul is writing to them, in a way, to say: "Stop crying or I'll give you something to cry about." He's saying, "You know people, things could be so much worse. What are you really whining about? What's the real problem here? Is it that you're frustrated with me, or is it that you aren't being cheerfully obedient to God. Because there's a huge difference between being obedient and *cheerfully* obedient."

Obedience is to follow the course of action prescribed by another. Cheerful obedience is to joyfully and willingly follow the course of action prescribed by another. You can be *begrudgingly* obedient. You can be *angrily* obedient. You can be *reluctantly* obedient. You can be *fearfully* obedient. But Paul calls us here to be *cheerfully* obedient no matter how easy or rough the conditions. Because, he reminds us, sooner or later we'll all have to face God, no matter what our conditions were like during our one-way journey on this celestial orb.

Paul calls us not to an obedience of begrudgement, anger, reluctance, or fear. Rather, he calls us to a cheerful obedience which flows from an intimate Love-relationship with God. Obedience out of begrudgement, anger, reluctance, or fear is a legalistic obedience—a religious obedience...following the rules so as not to get in trouble...or simply to get the grade. Cheerful obedience is to obey out of the Love you have for another—it is relational obedience...obeying because you Love the person and want to bring them pleasure.

God simply wants our Love. And when we fall in Love with God, we will come to know cheerful obedience.

My dad simply wanted my love, but as I was only a child, I didn't understand what it meant to obey him only because I Loved him. And so my dad would remind me of the consequences of my disobedience.

Because we are often as children to God, Paul reminds us here of the consequences of our disobedience: one day, we will stand before God in judgment. Paul reminds us a major part of our obedience is to urgently and vigilantly prepare others for the judgment they will one day face.

And the most basic element of our preparation is Loving God. And out of our Love, we will naturally be cheerfully obedient.

In a way, Paul is writing to the people of the church of Corinth as a daddy would discipline his children:

"Do I have to pull this church over? Because I will. I'll pull this church over and stop your ministry in front of God and everybody. Don't make me come back there to Corinth, people, because I will! If this church doesn't stop messin' around, I'll make your knees so red from praying so long you won't be able to kneel down until the Tuesday of next week. Oh yeah, and stop crying or I'll give you something to cry about. Things could be so much worse."

Yeah, our family trips were always an adventure. But eventually, we'd make it there. And eventually, we'd obey my father. And sometimes, we did need some reminders to be obedient.

Now that I'm a parent, I understand my father saying these things...in fact, I've even said some of my own versions of these at times to my own children.

God would like for our obedience to flow out of our Love for him, in the same way I'd like my children to be obedient out of their Love for me.

But occasionally, we're so caught up in ourselves: our wants and our "needs," that we can't see past our sin to see the Love. In some of these times, we need a not-so-gentle reminder of the judgment we will one day face.

All Bite And No Bark

Philippians 3:2-4

I will never forget the nasty Boston Terriers our neighbors, the Smileys (real name!) used to have. We used to live in a house right next door to the Smileys. From the age of four until I was seven years old, I dwelled within earshot of those nasty, fiendish, little beasts. Every day, when I was coming home from school, I would have to walk right by their house. And every day, there the little buggers were. To this day, when I see a Boston Terrier, thoughts of canicide fill my mind.

Here I am, a little six-year-old kid, coming home from school, minding my own business. I'm carrying my school bag filled with my *Tip and Mitten* book, three stubs of pencils, and the leftovers of my lunch in my Hong-Kong Phooey lunchbox. And there is the Smiley's house. It looms there ominously, like a haunted house up on the hill, housing the two monstrous predatory canines. I swear, that each day at 3:30 in the afternoon, the sky would turn to black, lightning would crackle down around me, and the very winds of Hades would whip up just to instill an even greater fear within my soul.

I would walk silently, tip-toeing my way towards my house that sat just beyond the Hell that was the Smiley's yard. I would creep closer and closer until... grrrrrrrr...what was that? Was that them? No, it was just the sound of a distant car...bark, bark, bark! Aaaaaaaaaahhhhhhhhh!!! And there they'd come, the hounds of Hell, flying down the hill of their front yard, snapping at my heels, barking all the way, chasing me right up to the front steps of my home where my mother would be waiting for me holding the door open, to then slam in the faces of those foul little beasts.

Each day would go by and I would be safe for another twenty-four hours.

You know, it was interesting, I was never bitten by those dogs. They would chase me every day, but never was I bitten by them. Oh sure, they snapped at my heels, but never did they really bite me.

The little Boston Terriers were more concerned with *appearing* to be ferocious, than with actually being ferocious. They were more concerned with barking and looking nasty, than with actually being nasty.

They filled the air with barking that had no real bite to it. *Their bark was much bigger than their bite.*

Do you know people of faith like this? They chase you around, telling you that you're not worthy, that you're not focusing on the proper things of the faith, when in actuality, it's difficult to discern what they see as important. They spend so much time decrying your cause that it becomes difficult to discern theirs. Or, they focus on one or two rules for the faith, forgetting the most basic parts of the faith, like Loving God and Loving people.

There are folks who focus on worship services who talk about the kinds of things we can and cannot do in worship and they spend so much time barking about worship, that the bite of their own worship becomes a mere snapping at the heels of God. There are folks who focus on "Christian" behavior who spend all their time barking about what we can and cannot do in our living, and forget to simply Love God everywhere and all of the time. There are those who bark and proclaim "Godly" visions of church buildings filled with people but forget the bite of the Good News of God's Love into someone's soul...the actual, transformational, life-changing Gospel of Jesus, which tells us that we are radically Loved by a Wild and Untamed God who not only barks his Love for us from the Heavens, but bites into our souls with Love, actually coming to earth to Love us in person.

God tells us to forget appearances here in this passage. We are told to focus on the actuality of who we are and how we're living. We are told to fill the air not with the empty barking of diluted theologies, but with the saturated praises of a Living God who promises New Life.

This passage from Paul to the church at Philippi tells us that there is a difference in those who believe: there are those who are all bark and no bite, and there are those who work away at the ministry, filling the air with God's Love. There are those who talk about "Godly" things who do not really Love God. And then there are those who talk about God, so that Godly things can be known. There are those who say they know God, who in reality haven't a clue. And then there are those who are in an intimate Love-relationship with God, spending every minute of every day with God.

These are the people who do not need to bark, because their bite is louder than their bark.

Do you Love God? Do you recognize God's constant presence in your life? Do you feel God's constant Love for you? Does God feel your constant Love for him? Do you proclaim "Godly" things but in reality have no idea who God is? Or do you know God so well, that by simply Loving God and those around you, Godly things are proclaimed in your living?

If you superficially know God and only guess at his Love for you, then you can only guess at what it means to live a God-honoring life. And your proclamations of

"Godly" living will be empty. Your bark will be louder than your bite.

But if you intimately Love Jesus with all your heart, then you will be one of those Paul talks about as "working away at this ministry, filling the air with Christ's praise." Because you will proclaim Godly living by living with God. Your bite will be louder than your bark.

Which is louder...your bark or your bite?

BAIT AND SWITCH

JUDE 1:3-4

For two "glorious" weeks of my existence, I sold a major brand name of vacuum cleaners door to door. I will not deceive you; they are good machines. They suck dirt from your basement right up through the floor of your main level. They are the workhorses of vacuum cleaners. They weigh a ton, but they're quality machinery providing quality service...and a good arm and back workout as well!

There are reasons that I only lasted two weeks selling vacuum cleaners. The first is that I was being sent into low-income neighborhoods to sell overpriced vacuum cleaners to people living off of Social Security and welfare. I wasn't even a Christian at the time and I had an ethical problem with this. The second reason is that the management pitted us against each other in competition to sell. There was no team aspect of sales. And the third reason I quit was the ol' bait & switch. We were trained to promise one thing, and deliver another.

When I arrived at a buyer's house, I would haul out not just a vacuum cleaner, but an entire house cleaning management system, complete with a carpet shampooer, stair-cleaner, and free gifts as well to entice them even further into signing over three months of their income. When I would enter, I would ask them to retrieve their pitiful, dilapidated vacuum cleaner from whatever exile of a closet they hid it in. They would then bring their vacuum proudly out into their living room upon which time I would strip them of all dignity as I began to unveil my house cleaning management system. By the time I was set up, my vacuum cleaner to theirs was like the Mall of America to a corner gas station. I would then systematically clean parts of their house exponentially greater than their pitiful excuse for a vacuum cleaner could ever do, further reducing them to the point of realizing that surely they must "*need*" such a machine as I was profferring.

Pretty soon, they would have their checkbook out and the deal was done. However, most of the people I sold to could not afford the entire house cleaning management system. And so to still make the sale, we would knock off parts of the system to get them down to a product they could afford more readily. And so, pretty soon, for most people anyway, no longer were they receiving the entire house cleaning management system, instead, all they were getting was a pretty nice vacuum cleaner. And what they would soon find out, is that without the whole house cleaning management system, their house would one day be only slightly cleaner than it was when I got there.

I offered them steak and gave 'em hot-dogs. Bait & switch. *Lies.*

Jude, in his letter to a group of believers, is warning of this bait and switch. There are men circulating amongst them who take the offer of God's Love and distort it...who cheapen it to make it affordable.

What these false teachers are offering is cheap love...no capital L. Not the Love of God shown in the forgiveness of our sins, even though we don't deserve it. But God clearly requires repentance...a changing of our lives to match the way of life that shows our Love for God. And all repentance means is to turn away from something. It's not a shaming. In Matthew 4:17, it says "Jesus started preaching. He picked up where John left off: 'Change your life. God's kingdom is here.'" In other words, repent...turn away from the Love-less life you are living and live a life that shows your Love for God and others in all you say and do.

These false teachers were telling the people, "Go for it! Go and party. Go and gratify the desires of your flesh. Because it doesn't matter. It's only your body. And God is Spirit...and will forgive you no matter what, right? So, sin today, ask for forgiveness tomorrow. Bada-bing, bada-boom. There ya go."

And Jude is saying in response, "Nuh uh. These guys are wrong. God's Love without repentance is cheap and unworthy of our great and Loving God. You can't live a life which honors God and continue to willfully walk in sin, disregarding God's heart. Because you know what...if you cheapen God's Love like this, you're basically saying that you don't need God. You have no need for a Savior. And my friends, guess what...you do have a need for a Savior. Big time. And so do I.

Paul writes to the church at Rome, "For what I do is not the good I want to do; no, the evil I do not want to do—this I keep on doing. Now if I do what I do not want to do, it is no longer I who do it, but it is sin living in me that does it." Romans 7:19-20 In other words, "I try not to sin...but I continue to do so...even when I don't want to." Paul reminds us here of our need for a Savior.

I went to seminary being told that I would learn more about who God was and how much I needed God in my life and how best to communicate the Gospel to a congregation. It ain't what I got. In the seminary I attended, I was told that I didn't need Jesus. I was told that all I had to do was make good choices in my life and that would be my salvation. But you know what? Just like Paul, "I try not to sin...but I continue to do so...even when I don't want to!"

I need a Savior...and so do you.

And anyone who tells you differently is telling you a lie.

Jesus offers us a house cleaning management system...and he follows through with his promise. He helps us to get our spiritual houses clean, so that he can take up residence there and make our hearts his home. He does not offer us a cheapened version...a stripped-down model trying to make it affordable to us. He holds a high standard out of his Love for us.

God's Love without repentance...forgiveness without a turning away from the sin is a cheap substitution for what Jesus offers. It's attractive, to be sure...but it ain't what Jesus offers. And anything other than what Jesus offers will one day leave your house even dirtier than it was before.

Unless you get the whole house cleaning management system, you will end up with nothing more than a glorified vacuum cleaner and a dirty house.

Unless you get the Grace Jesus offers, complete with repentance, you will end up with nothing more than a glorified religion and a sin-filled soul.

Don't fall for the ol' bait & switch, my friends. Take the real deal. Jesus...his Love...and a life of repentance.

And so I write to you today, my friends, in the same way Jude wrote to the church he cared so deeply for to tell you to "fight with everything you have in you for this faith entrusted to us as a gift to guard and cherish." Do not let others cheapen it and offer you a faith that doesn't need God's Love.

The Faith in us and the Love God offers are precious beyond price.

Let's not let that be cheapened by anyone. God offers and delivers the whole deal...no bait and switch. And we receive the whole deal when we receive God's Love, and then return that Love to God, and to those around us.

WHERE YOU LEAD, PEOPLE FOLLOW

JOHN 18:17-18, 25-27

I relate to Peter so well. Of all the characters in the Bible, besides Jesus, of course, Peter is my favorite. He's fiery. Bold. Peter is a leader. And here in this passage, look at where he leads...

Peter denies his best friend, Jesus. Three times he denies Jesus...three times, he leads people away from Jesus. Because that's what he's doing. Peter is a leader by nature, and here he leads people away from Jesus by denying him.

The first denial. It came quickly, almost without thinking. "Aren't you?" asks the woman. "No!" Peter vehemently says. People around him are struggling to get close to the fire to stay warm. Peter stands there blindly staring into the flames...past them...into the deepest parts of his soul. He thinks to himself, "Why did I just say that? How could I do that to my best friend? How could I do that to God? I'm a terrible friend...a terrible student. I'll never deny him again. I'll change. God I'm sorry. You'll see...I'll be diff..."

The second denial comes after a sharp intake of breath, holding it for half a second, as if Peter is going to say the right thing, the truthful thing...but then comes the denial. "You must have mistaken me for somebody else." The man who asked him is still looking at him quizzically, pretty sure that Peter is one of Jesus' friends...but having no proof, he can only sit there and wonder...what if?

The third denial is poignant, because in it are two lies: "Hey, wasn't that you who cut off my cousin's ear? Aren't you one of his disciples?" With half a faked laugh, Peter says: "You know, I must have a twin around here or something! People keep asking me if I know Jesus. Sure, I've heard of the guy. Who hasn't? But his friend? Please. You've got to be kidding. That guy's a..." Peter thinks a novel in this second-long pause {"The guy is my best friend. He's my Savior. He's your Savior. And if you only knew him...your life would change...you would change."} "That guy's a lunatic."

And the gavel of the rooster's crow slams down upon the dawn.

And Peter stands there guilty, even as his Friend and Savior stands being judged by the Chief Priest.

Peter, a leader by nature, leads people away from Jesus. Not to protect Jesus, but to protect himself. I've tried to re-read this and make Peter an undercover hero acting with Jesus' best interests at heart. But I can only come up with cowardice each time I read this.

Peter has three chances to share the Savior with three people who need to hear about him, and instead of taking them to the Savior's feet, he leads them as far away from Jesus as east is from west. Which is as far as Jesus takes our sins away from us when we are forgiven.

The people Peter could have shared Jesus with...what were they doing around that fire so late at night...so early in the morning? Where were their families? The woman at the door...what about her? Could it be, that she asked Peter about Jesus, because she had seen him one day in the streets, healing people, laughing with children and she wondered who this man could be and why people whispered "Messiah" when he was around? Could it be that she wanted to know if the rumors were true so that she could somehow try to help Peter...or maybe even help Jesus? Could it be that the man at the fire was looking for something to warm his soul and not just his body? Could it be that he was just a lonely man who had lost his family to illness and ended up here at this small fire, huddled before it, trying to hold the tears back so that no one would see his hurt? Could it be that Peter denied this man the one Answer that would satisfy all of his longings? And could it be that the servant, the cousin of the man whose ear Peter cut off, simply wanted to know why? Could it be that he too had heard of the gentle man known as Jesus, who taught things which made his master angry, but made him laugh? Could it be that he just wanted to know why a follower of a guy like Jesus would behave in such a way, cutting off his cousin's ear? Could it be that he just wanted to understand...maybe even just to listen?

But Peter never gave them a chance. Peter, to the best of his leadership ability, led them in the opposite direction...away from his Savior...away from *their* Savior.

Each time we sin...each time we live a life that does not reflect God's Love, we are like Peter, denying Jesus...leading people away from their Savior. How are you like Peter? How are you leading people away from their Savior? How do you deny Jesus? Do you deny him in your thoughts? How do you deny him through the things you do? Do you deny him at work, pretending that you're just like everybody else...that you're not a "religious freak?" Do you deny him in your family, never taking the time to pray with your spouse or your children? Do you deny him daily, or just when it's convenient?

I'm pretty sure I deny Jesus more often than I care to admit...but the thing is, I have to admit it. I have to admit my denials, because they are my sins...and we are called to confess our sins. In James 5:16, it says: "Make this your common practice: Confess your sins to each other and pray for each other so that you can live together whole and healed."

I confess my sins. I confess that I have not Loved God with all of my heart, nor all of my mind, nor all my strength, nor with all of my soul. I confess that I have not Loved my neighbor as myself. I sometimes don't even Love my spouse as myself, let alone my children. I confess that I have idolized things and people and not given all of my Love to God. I confess that I tend to rely more on my own strength and power, than God's.

I confess today that I have denied Jesus...that I have led people away from my Savior...from *their* Savior.

And the gavel of my shame slams down upon my sins for I am guilty.

And so are you each time you deny Jesus...each time you sin.

But that's not the end of the story...because it says in 1 John 1:9-10 "If we confess our sins, he who is faithful and just and will forgive us our sins and purify us from all unrighteousness. If we claim we have not sinned, we make him out to be a liar and his word has no place in our lives."

If we confess our Jesus-denials, our sins, Jesus will forgive us and cleanse us.

When we deny Jesus, we are the liars. When we deny our sins, we make Jesus the liar for it is Jesus who tells us, "Whoever believes in me will have eternal life."

Where will you lead people today? Will you lead them closer to God's Love or further away? Will your life point the way to Love? Will your life point the way to God?

Where you lead, people follow. Lead them to Jesus...they're dying for you to.

BREATHE ON ME

ROMANS 8:1-2

I went to college in Moorhead, Minnesota at a small Lutheran school. Moorhead is a wonderful place to live in the summer as the winter months can be brutal. But worse than all of the snow and cold, the winters in Moorhead brought us a stench that constantly hovered over the town. You could always tell when winter officially started by the rank, odiferous bouquet of foul-scented pungency which would encroach upon the town towards the end of each autumn.

This smell signaled the beginning of the sugar beet refining process. Ah yes, this lovely area is home to a sugar beet plant where they process sugar beets to make sugar. And this process stinks. It's not the kind of stink where you gag and choke. It's the kind of stink which is a constant annoyance, like a mosquito buzzing in your ear.

Isn't it interesting that something which tastes so sweet is so stinky to make?

Kind of like sin, huh?

Sin so often tastes so sweet, but it creates a stench. And the stench follows us wherever we go. It's always there, constantly nagging at us until it is cleared away. And it nags at those around us, who can smell the effects of sin in our lives as well. They smell it, having to put up with it until it is taken care of.

But, when the springtime came, and the winds began to blow from the south, the stench was carried away. And our nostrils would rejoice doing a little happy dance as once again, pure air once again graced our nasal passages. We would go outside and say to each other, "Do you smell that?" "What?" someone would always ask. "Exactly!" We'd say. "There's nothing to smell! Isn't it wonderful?!"

Paul, in his letter to the church at Rome, tells them that the Spirit of Life that is in Jesus does exactly that for us: it clears the air. It blows away the stench of sin, the malodorous smell of death. It's a southern wind, breathing life into us, forcing us to exhale the evil we've taken in. It's a southern wind blowing away the low-lying black cloud of sin-stink in which we've come to dwell.

And no matter how hard we try, we cannot leave the smell behind. In college, there was nowhere we could go in town to escape the smell of sugar beets being refined into sugar. It was everywhere. And so it is in life, there is nowhere we can go to leave behind the sin-stink which is around us...because we are its source. The sin-stink emanates from us. Wherever we go, so does the stench of our sin. We can do nothing about it.

But Jesus can.

Jesus breathes the Spirit of Life into us. Jesus breathes fresh air into our lives. Jesus breathes a New Power which is able to carry away the effects of sin and death. And this New Power that he breathes is called Love...and it smells fresh like spring. In the Song of Songs 2:11-12, we find the kind of intimate relationship God wants to have with us. God says to us "Look around you: Winter is over; the winter rains are over, gone! Spring flowers are in blossom all over."

My friends, when Jesus breathes the Spirit of Life, he's blowing away the sin-stink that comes with the dead winter of our lives. And he's breathing the Spirit of Life into us...he's breathing spring into us. And the flowers

and New Life which come with spring smell a lot differently than does the stink of our sinful winter.

Wherever you are right now, stop and breathe in. Take
a deep spiritual breath...in through your nose...out
through your mouth. How does it smell? Are you smelling
the effects of sin and death in your life? Have you let
Jesus into your life so that he can breathe New Life into
you? Have you let him close enough to blow away the low-
lying black cloud of sin-stink which is emanating from
you? Because only he can do it. There is nowhere you can
go to get away from it...except into the arms of God. Only
God can take the stench away. Only God can take your
sins away. Only he can give you New Life through the New
Power which only he can breathe into your existence.

We sing a song in worship which has lyrics that will be
our prayer for today:
Breathe on me.
Breathe on me.
Holy Spirit Power, come breathe on me.
Yesterday's gone. Today I'm in need.
Holy Spirit Power, come breathe on me.
—Clint Brown

Breathe on us, Lord Jesus. Breathe Your New Power into
our lives. Clear away the stench of our sin. And replace it
with the Glorious scent of your Love. Amen.

GETTING AWAY WITH IT

JOHN 6:70-71

When you were in school, did you ever do something to get yourself in trouble, but didn't get caught? I remember one time in 6th grade, in Mrs. Satre's class, this one girl and I had a spitball fight. A big one. In fact, we were chewing up entire pieces of notebook paper to throw at each other. Besides being pretty darn gross...it was also a lot of fun. That is, until one of our shots went astray and Mrs. Satre finally noticed that something was going on.

"Okay. That's enough! I've had it up to here." (She never did indicate where "here" was.) "Who is throwing spitballs in my classroom?"

Everybody sat there silently.

"Who is the guilty party? Who made this mess? Tell me, who!?!?" Her ire was peaking.

And I sat there with a silent war raging in my head. "Should I admit it? Nah. She won't find out. But what if she already knows? Won't it be better for me if I just admit it? What's the right thing to do? Who cares?! She'll never find out. Nobody will talk...b..but what if they do? Then I'll really get it. Oh man...what should I do?"

At the time, we were greatly thankful that our class-mates did not betray us. We all sat there silently, waiting for the storm to blow over. It did. Mrs. Satre went back to teaching us some other interesting fact about the English language.

I remember in that moment, that I did not feel smug. Actually, I felt guilty. I knew that everyone else around me knew who was throwing spitballs. And the one person who actually should have known didn't. I was afraid she'd find out. I was afraid she'd have some serious consequences for me. I was afraid and guilty.

I imagine that at that moment when Jesus said, "Still, one of you is a devil," that Judas was feeling similarly. I imagine that he was afraid. I imagine that he was feeling guilty. His situation, however, was a bit reversed from mine. In my situation, the whole class knew, but the teacher did not. In Judas' situation, the class did not know, but the Teacher did.

I wonder if Judas knew, that Jesus knew. I imagine Judas sitting there imagining all sorts of scenarios and being filled with paranoia. I imagine the war which raged on inside his head as Jesus told them that one of them is a devil.

"I wonder if he knows it's me? What am I going to do? Okay, get a grip Judas. Hold it together. Just a little while longer and it's a done deal. But look at the way he's looking at me...He must know it's me. No, no...He couldn't. How could he? Breathe. Don't make eye contact again. Judas, all you're doing is telling them which one Jesus is so they get the right guy. It's not like you're killing him or anything. Hasn't he caused you enough trouble? Yeah, there's been trouble...but...well, I love the guy. And...well...I don't know. I don't want to...but I *have* to."

I imagine that Judas has a heart. I imagine that Judas was ripped up inside about this. I imagine that Judas quickly wiped a tear away so that no one would see and suspect it was him. But I imagine the tear was there. And that it trickled slowly down his face as he looked into the eyes of his friend. Because I also imagine that he knew...that he suspected...that his action...that simple kiss...would snowball into absolute betrayal.

Jesus looked out over his Twelve...his closest friends...his students and he knew that one of them would betray him. In fact, he knew which one. And here, he gives Judas a chance to 'fess up. But Judas doesn't take it. He lets it play through, just like I did in Mrs. Satre's classroom.

I got away with it.

So did Judas.

What have you gotten away with? What have you packed down deep inside the furthest recesses of your being that still gnaws at you? What are the things you've done which make you like Judas?

Everyday, Jesus gives us a chance to 'fess up. Take him up on it. Tell him the things you've done which you've "gotten away with." Ask him for forgiveness. Take it a step further, if it makes sense to make restitution with someone without causing them too much emotional damage, call up the person and tell them. 'Fess up. Apologize. Get things right between you...and between you and God.

Judas never did this. And his guilt consumed him to the point where he could take it no longer. He was so filled with shame, guilt, and pain that he took his own life.

I wish Judas had stuck around a little longer. Because then he'd know the rest of the story. He'd know about Hope. He'd know about Grace. He'd know that there's always a chance to 'fess up. He'd know the kind of Love that God has for him and that God's Love is bigger than all of our sins. God's Love is even bigger than betrayal. God's Love can take it.

Did Judas really get away with it?

Let's let God be the judge of that.

I should call Mrs. Satre.

ATTENTION DEFICIT

LUKE 13:23-24

In high school, I had one of those teachers who knew everything he needed to know about his subject, felt the passion for the subject in his soul, but couldn't convey that knowledge in a way that a South American tree-sloth would find interesting. If you know who Ben Stein is, you've got a clue as to the level of interest this man can maintain. Watching the grass grow would hold far greater levels of excitement than his teaching. He brings whole new levels of meaning to the word "monotone." His voice was about as interesting as the tone they play for the Emergency Broadcast System. Nothing stood out about this man. He wore almost the exact same suit and tie every day with only slight variations. His hair was combed the same way. His glasses were the same. His lectures were the same...well, they seemed that way.

I can't count the number of times I was caught lost in some world other than his classroom. "Shane, can you tell me who the first Pony Express rider was?" And as I'd wipe the drool from the corner of my mouth and the sleep from my eyes, I would stammer forth with an intelligent: "Pony Express? Huh?"

There was certainly a deficit of my attention in his class.

Until the last day of school, my senior year.

He was dressed as usual. And he began his class as usual. Yes, *the last day of school*, he wanted to deliver another stimulating lecture on some aspect of government history. As he started into his talk, he reached up and loosened his tie just a little bit. Then after a while, he unbuttoned the top button of his shirt. With this action, he began to draw our attention. After a few minutes, he took off his tie. Now we were listening...in reality, we were watching his every move at this point.

I can't tell you a thing he said that day. But I will never forget the progression of events which ensued. His passion began to show and he became a little more animated. He then removed his sport-coat. By this time, the whole class began to nervously look at each other. But our eyes never strayed from him for more than a passing glance to our neighbor, so enrapt were we. With about ten minutes left in the class, he took off his white buttoned-down shirt. Our mouths hung open as he stood there teaching in his dress pants, white t-shirt, and dress shoes. With only minutes left, he stopped, turned to face us directly, and he began to undo his belt, and then dropped his pants.

A gasp of pure terror escaped from each mouth at the thought that we were about to see our monotonous educator standing in front of us in his knickers.

He was wearing shorts underneath his pants. We didn't see his undies. Thank God, for I'm sure we'd all have fainted dead away at the sight. With this final action, our normally dry, completely un-funny teacher doubled over laughing hysterically. He quickly re-dressed and as the bell rang, he put his finger up to his lips and simply whispered "Shhhhh."

This was the one moment this man lived for. I almost believe that the only reason he taught was for this moment each year. One moment of complete hilarity. One class taught with our total attention...all eyes affixed to his every move. One moment without any deficit of attention.

Unfortunately, this is how our walk of faith often ends up: one brief moment of God having our total attention. Instead of each day having our complete attention, like my poor teacher, God only occasionally enjoys our partial attention...let alone our total attention.

But here, as Jesus talks to a passer-by, he reminds us that the way to his daddy requires our eyes being completely fixed on God. Jesus, the Way to God, requires our total attention. We're not to worry about who's going to get to go to Heaven. We're simply supposed to keep our eyes fixed on God. We're not to worry about what we're supposed to eat or drink or wear. We're supposed to keep our eyes on God. We're not to spend our time with silly arguments which distract others from God. We're supposed to give God our total and complete attention.

Tall order. But is God anything like my monotonous teacher? Is God that un-funny? Is God that uninteresting? Is it that big of a challenge for God to hold our attention? It shouldn't be. But so often, we think that we're so much more funny...so much more interesting. So often we think there are more important things to which to give our attention than Jesus.

Jesus, told the best stories, the funniest jokes, and could capture the attention of literally thousands of people for hours at a time. Jesus didn't have to do what my teacher did to get our attention. He could simply open his mouth, and out would come words spoken with such passion that it became nigh impossible to devote your attention to anyone or anything else but him. Imagine being in the presence of Jesus. Imagine hearing his sermon on the mount. Imagine him stopping to tell parables to the Pharisees. Imagine him stopping to talk with the children. Imagine being at the last supper.

Everywhere Jesus went, he did not lack for peoples' attention.

Except that last night in the Garden at Gethsemane. And this is where he knew once and for all that he would have to go the way of the cross. He asked for the cup to pass from him. He asked for another way. But his daddy knew this was the only way and told him so.

The cross was the only way to get rid of the deficit of our attention. It was the one moment that Jesus lived for...and *died* for.

The cross was the only way to catch peoples' attention for all of time. It was the last lesson before the bell would ring on history. But this time, at the end of class, Jesus did not tell us to "shhh." This time, Jesus told us to get out there and tell everyone. This final attention-grabbing lesson was no secret to be hidden from the next unsuspecting students. Rather, it was the lesson we are to proclaim to everyone. It is the lesson of love. It is the lesson of Grace. It is the most-attention-getting lesson of all of time.

Who or what has your attention today? Does Jesus? Does he have a deficit of your attention?

Turn your eyes upon Jesus,
Look full in his wonderful face,
And the things of earth will grow strangely dim
In the light of his glory and grace.
—Helen H. Lemmel, 1922

YOU'RE DRAWING ATTENTION!

MATTHEW 6:1-5

Third grade. Mrs. Lundquist. She was a dear woman with a lot of patience for those who wanted to learn and be in her classroom. For those who didn't, watch out. One of Mrs. Lundquist's goals for her students was to have them learn their multiplication tables all the way through 12. 12 x 1...12 x 2...12 x 3...etc.

When I had Mrs. Lundquist, I was one of the children who wanted to be there. I wanted to learn. I loved learning. And I loved those multiplication tables. I would practice them on the bus ride home from school. I knew them backwards, forwards, and inside-out. They didn't even have to be in order. But when they were, that made it that much easier for me...to win that is.

You see, in regards to the multiplication tables, not only did I want to know them...but I also had to be the fastest and the best at knowing them. Only once or twice did I slip from first place in the multiplication table test. Most of the time, I was the first one done and had them all right. I loved seeing the little "100%" mark with the smiley face that Mrs. Lundquist would put on my paper. But even more than that, I loved the satisfaction of being done first. I loved the looks I would get from those around me. Looks of awe, recognition, and envy. I lived for those days when we would do the multiplication table test. Because on those days, I would be recognized by everyone in my class. Fame. Glory!

<POP!> Okay, it's time to burst my own bubble here. "Get a grip, Shane, it was a third-grade test, for crying out loud!"

"Yeah, but the feel of that recognition was so sweet."

Maybe about as sweet as someone walking up to you while you're praying and saying, "Wow, I envy your discipline." Or they see you reading your Bible in a public place and say, "I wish I had the guts to do that." Or maybe someone at work notices you saying grace before you eat your sack lunch from home, "That's very cool that you say grace for your bag lunch!" And it feels good, doesn't it? Be honest. When someone notices you practicing your faith, it feels really good. You walk a little taller. You hold your chin up a little higher. And with great boldness, you continue praying or reading the Bible, secretly hoping that someone else will stop by and further stroke your ego.

<POP!> Now it's time for God to burst both our bubbles! Because that's exactly what Jesus is saying we should not do here in this passage of Scripture from the Sermon on the Mount. First of all, he's telling us that we shouldn't make a show out of our spiritual life at all. It's one thing to be sitting in public and reading Scripture, it's quite another to do it on purpose. It's one thing to get to worship early to pray, but an entirely different thing to do so hoping that your pastor will notice how spiritual you are. It's one thing to give more money in the offering plate because you've gotten a bonus at work, and an entirely different thing to give extra, laying the check right on top, unfolded so that those after you will see how much you gave. It's one thing to take a day of fasting telling a few trusted friends so they hold you accountable, and quite another thing to fast and then ask people out to dinner so you can tell them why you're not eating.

Here's the difference: the first way helps you to focus your attention on Loving God...and Loving people, while the second focuses all the attention on yourself.

As one who knows, it's not always a good idea to have the attention drawn to yourself. For while you may do some great things occasionally, there will come a time when you will do something either embarrassing or sinful or both and everybody's eyes will be on you. For when we sin, it is out of our woundedness, and we were created in such a way as to self-destruct in such times, outing ourselves in those moments to get help...to *heal*. So rather than do that, just get the help you need to heal and you will begin to see a lot less mess in your life.

There's an even greater reason to not draw all of the attention to yourself: and that is because God desires our Love...and for us to Love others. Not so God can be center -stage and bask in the glory. But because God Loves us and hopes that we feel the same way.

When we feel this need to draw all of the attention to ourselves, we negate the sacred worth given to us in our relationship with God. We try to find our worth in places, people, and things other than God. And when we do this, we turn our backs on the worth given to us through God's Love...a worth more valuable than all of the opinions of all of the people who have ever lived, or ever will live on this planet.

If you feel the need to draw attention, just make sure God is drawing yours first.

All the recognition you will ever need will be when Jesus calls you out of the line-up of the ages and recogniz-es you as one of his. That's better than any pat on the back, prize, fame, glory, or standing ovation.

Whose attention are you drawing to what or to whom today? Does God have your attention? My friend, know that you have God's. God says that his eye is on the sparrow...and that he watches over you even more than the sparrow. I pray that your attention is drawn to God today...and that any attention you draw would be to God. And I pray for your recognition, that one day, Jesus will pull you out of the line-up of the ages saying, "Well done, my good and faithful servant!"

It's all the recognition you'll ever need!

THIS IS TO MY DADDY'S GLORY

JOHN 15:1-9

To describe the vine as lush would be a disservice. A vibrant life force coursed through the xylem and phloem of this plant. Its leaves were not only a hearty green, but they were broader than a large man's hands, fingers splayed. Near each leaf there were small, coiled tendrils, stretching...searching for their next purchase, desperate to get to their next zenith. As I observed the vine, I could not help but to wonder at its aesthetic beauty. This vine was vast in its growth and there seemed no end to it.

Nor could I see its beginning. From whence did such a vine as this originate? As long as I sat there, I could not see it. I could not find its origin. The ends of those desperate tendrils were distant from the original vine. And yet, they groped, persistently and somewhat obnoxiously. For while they were filled with life, they were also taking life in the process. Those same verdant tendrils were literally strangling the life from several trees.

The branches on this vine had grown unchecked.

No gardener was present, caring for this vine. No nurturing spirit guiding, helping, or pruning could be found except its own willful, aimless independence.

In stark contrast to the life of this vine and its branches was its utter lack of fruit. I sat studying the branches of this vine for nigh unto an hour and could not find the vestiges of one grape.

If you were to take a look today at your life...a branch on the Vine that is Jesus, what would you see?

Would you see a wild, reckless branch, tendrils groping aimlessly and desperately, trying to prove that you can make it on your own? You don't need anyone, do you? In fact, nobody is going to come along and prune you. At first glance, are you a marvel to behold, but upon closer inspection, your true purpose is, at best, unrealized?

At times, I have been this kind of a branch on the True Vine of Jesus. At times, I have held to my pride as my motivation to keep going. And I have pushed so hard, so long...so far...that eventually I had grown myself a great distance from God. And in those times, all I could think to do was to keep growing and grasping, groping for some vestige of Hope. Have you been this branch? *Are* you this branch? As you gaze at your form, do you see lush leaves, and yet no fruit? Are you reading this now realizing that you are too far away from God, living life solo? Stop. You don't have to do this alone. In fact, you don't have to do anything...the True Vine already did it for you. It is done. "It is finished," said one Carpenter. A warning friend: even if you have the lushest of leaves, but bear no fruit, you will be pruned from the Vine altogether and thrown into the fire. You will be given chance after chance to surrender to the ministrations of the Gardener. But in the end, it will come down to your choice of whether or not you let him take away your sin, or force him to prune you from the Vine entirely.

Or maybe you are a branch whose leaves are withered. You're dying, wasting away, your life force waning. Your leaves are almost dry to the touch. The dank smell of decay hangs about you like dirty clothes pulled from the laundry room. You know better, and yet you put them on anyway. Your leaves are withering because you are not getting any sustenance, or worse, that which you are ingesting is poison. What is the make up of your diet? What do you ingest with your ears, your eyes, your mind, your stomach? What is in your spiritual diet? Do you take in your "nutrition" from Chinese year placemats at the local take-out? Do you scan the pages of the "entertainment" section of your newspaper, looking for your month...your sign, desperate for Hope? Do you go to a church which preaches Jesus crucified, but not physically resurrected? These are empty promises, friend. It is no wonder you wither. If you watch poison, listen to poison, ponder poison, and digest poison, what do you expect the effects to be? If your diet is sin, what are its wages?

Of course...death. An excruciating, monotonously lonely death, devoid of meaning. You will have withered to the point of death, and you too, will be thrown into the fire. It's time to check your diet and start putting in the right stuff. It will take time for your withered branch to work out the poison and its effects, but you will begin to feel it immediately. Turn off the porn...and for that matter, don't look twice at the pretty girl or the hot guy in the car next to you. Censor your music...ask yourself, would I play this if God were driving...or your children...or your Grandma? Guard your thoughts...for whatever you think, it is as if you have done it. And try a vegetable once in a while...physical health is important! And for your own sake, find a church which preaches a God of Love.

Or maybe today, you're checking yourself out in your spiritual mirror and you do have fruit. Your branches are healthy. You're growing in healthy ways. But as you look more closely, some of your tiny tendrils, ones you try to hide, are still untamed, groping for the seediest of purchases. Under the cover of some of your leaves and bunches of fruit, you have hidden away secret tendrils, still clutching onto sinful purchases in the darkness.

At some time or another, I'm sure we are all this branch. In the darkness, we still send out little feelers into the realm of sin. We covet a nice car. We lust after someone with our eyes...or worse, with our hearts. We engage in practices under cover which we hope—for we dare not pray—will never be uncovered.

I know that in some way, I fall into this category. I know there are impure thoughts I have...and deeds I've done. I know that I continue, despite my best efforts, to sin, and even sometimes willfully. Because I have wounds. And so do you. And these wounds left untended tend to come out sideways. And thus, we sin.

Here is something not commonly known about the garden in which we grow: to be pruned, we must invite the Gardener. He stands at the gate of our garden...our heart...and he knocks. Ultimately, it is we who must invite him to do his work. At times it will hurt, but with the healing there is always some pain. God will, as gently as possible, prune away those sinful tendrils of ours. To prune is to cut, ergo there is pain. But where the pruning has taken place, the possibility for abundant fruit becomes a reality. For it is only when we are kept in check, when we are kept close to our origin, the True Vine, that we can truly bear much fruit.

And when it does...when you do...when we do...we will bear much fruit! We will attest to the greatness of God, our True Vine. We will become a living witness and sacrifice of praise! We will proclaim with our very lives, "This is to my Daddy's glory!" In short, we will live lives of Love.

If you are the lush vine devoid of fruit, *surrender*.

If you are the withering vine, *repent*.

If you are the last vine, *invite*.
This is to our Daddy's glory, friends.

You are the Vine,
Taking root in our lives.
We are the branches,
Bearing New Life,
To those who don't know,
To those who don't shine.
We are the branches.
But You are the Vine.

You are the Vine,
Taking root in our lives.
We are the branches,
Bearing New Life.
By this My Daddy,
Is glorified,
You bear the fruit,
Of New Life.
—Shane Allen Burton

MOUNTAINS INTO MOLE HILLS

2 CORINTHIANS 4:1-2, 16-19

I have taken several groups of youth on mission trips into the hills and hollers of the Appalachian mountains in Tennessee. Each trip has been an adventure! On one trip, we were almost ran off the road by an overzealous trucker who didn't like us "Yanks." On another trip, I was struck by lightning. And on another trip, we almost had to quit.

The troubles started before we ever left. The cost of taking a mission trip is quite high, actually. We had to raise more than $15,000 to go on this trip. And we were cutting it close. As of the week before the trip, we didn't have enough to go. But God provided for us. Some donations came in and we did a couple of last minute fund-raisers and God provided what we needed.

We also had a difficult time finding vehicles to take on the trip. Not too many people want you to take their van for a week and a half into Tennessee as a work vehicle filled with teenagers. For many people, allowing such usage would be like inviting a herd of yaks into their living rooms. Again, at the last minute, God provided the necessary vehicles.

And one of them only lasted us about three hundred miles into the trip. We got about two-thirds of the way through Wisconsin and one of our minivans died. We brought it to Sal at the local repair shop and of course, the part needed could only be special-ordered from a small place in Virginia. This is no exaggeration! It would take until Tuesday to get the part. It was Thursday. We couldn't wait until then.

The temperature was hot. Tempers were flaring. Morale was low. Mutiny was in the air. I feared for my life.

Until we prayed.

We got all twenty-nine of us together in a circle and we prayed. We prayed for God's leading. We prayed for help. We prayed for our mission. And we decided to go for it!

With a new enthusiasm, we re-distributed the bodies between the vehicles, squeezed in like clowns in circus-car -minivans, and we headed off towards our mission field.

Do you ever despair? Do you ever get so caught up in the pitfalls of your present circumstances that you just feel like cashin' in your chips and headin' for home? I can relate. There have been times in my life when all I knew was headache and heartache. There have been times when I've been so enmeshed in my tribulations, that I've forgotten about the source of my salvation. There have been times in the midst of difficulty and poverty that I've forgotten about my eternity. It is only when I've forgotten about God in my life that I've come to despair. It's only when I've come to the point of self-reliance, that I've found myself grasping for something or someone to rely upon.

Paul writes in his second letter to the church at Corinth to encourage. He tells them to hold their course. Keep preaching the Good News of God's Love. Don't soften it. Don't water it down. Don't change it at all to cater to the whims of the powers-that-be. He's telling them that life will sometimes suck...ministry will some-times be an uphill battle against impossible odds. And he's telling that it's cool, because their current struggle is nothing compared to the party that awaits them.

Are you struggling with anything today? Does despair sit waiting on your doorstep? Are you tempted to give up...or give in? Are you struggling with a friendship? Are the bills piling up? Is your marriage going through hard times? Are there challenges within your church? Are you experiencing persecution for your faith?

Oh, my gosh, I have been there, friend. Big time. Huge. I have walked in difficult places and have at least somewhat of an understanding of what it means to go through the valley. Alienation from family and friends? Been there. On the verge of financial ruin? Done that one too. Marriage troubles. Hey, I'm on marriage number four. And I own my part in the demise of each. I don't recount my troubles for any sort of pity or simply to make you feel better about your own. But rather, to point the way to Faith and healing.

All of these are things in our lives which can tempt us to despair. Things on the outside may look bleak in some aspect of your life. But do not give up! How could you? God is with you. And if God is with you, truly, my friend, who can stand against you? Be true to God's leading of your life. Be true to Loving God and Loving others. Listen to God's voice for your life.

Stop. Take a deep breath. Exhale. Do it again. Now, let's take an inventory. Do you know who you are? You are a son or daughter of the King of Kings. You are a co-heir with Jesus. The Lion of Judah walks at your side! You will one day be seated at the right hand of God along with the Son! Imagine what your current trials would look like if you remembered that you are a prince or princess in the Kingdom of God. You are royalty. From this vantage point, the current mountains of your existence will one day be shown to be the mole hills they really are in comparison to the true Mountain that is God and the lavish celebration that awaits when you come into your inheritance in the Kingdom!

MOCK WORSHIP

MARK 15:16-20

I wonder what Jesus was thinking as he saw these war-scarred soldiers mockingly worshiping him? Huge men, each of them stronger than probably anyone you know, wearing plates of bronze as a part of their uniforms, able to wield fifty pound swords, and there they are, kneeling in the dirt at Jesus' feet. I imagine them sarcastically kneeling there, raising their arms up and down, saying, "We're not worthy!"

Did Jesus scoff at them? Was he angry? When they hit him with the club, and then did about the lowest thing you can do to a person: spit on him, was Jesus ever tempted to dip into the God-head for a dash of omnipotence to send down a lightning bolt or two?

Did any of these soldiers feel any remorse for their actions? Were any of them ashamed when they wrote their letters home to their families that night? "My Dearest Family, you should be proud of daddy. Today we took an innocent man, and we dressed him up as a false king and then beat him, whipped, him, and spit upon him. We teased him and mocked him in front of all of his friends and family. And, get this, to top it all off...we nailed him to a cross! Aren't you proud of your daddy? I'll bet you want to grow up to be just like me! I'll be home next month. All of my love."

Did any of these soldiers go along with this simply because of peer-pressure? Did they simply join in the teasing because they didn't want to bear the responsibility and burden of sticking up for the innocent man they tortured? Did they join in so they wouldn't stick out? Did they join in because of the cowardice smoldering in their hearts...a cowardice which always prevented them from doing the right thing in the face of adversity?

I wonder which one of these soldiers was the one who said: "Truly this man was the Son of God." How did he live with himself after this? How did he justify his actions? Did he continue in service to Rome? Or did he quietly slip away, gather up his family, and set off to start a new life...the new life that was purchased for him by the man he just helped nail to the cross? Did he ever know? Did he ever know what had truly happened on that cross that day? Did he ever come to that soul-knowledge of the nature of the entire universe being changed through those nails that he helped to drive through human flesh? Did he ever understand the covenant that was completed, the prophecies that were fulfilled, and the Grace that was made available that day?

Oh, I hope so. I hope this man who realized the identity of the man he had just nailed to the cross didn't just know the identity...but also believed it in his heart. He stood there that day and when Jesus died, right before his eyes, he proclaimed loudly enough for many to hear that day, otherwise we would not have this statement recorded in Scripture, "This has to be the Son of God." He confessed Jesus with his mouth. All that was left was for him was to believe it in his heart. I hope and pray that one day I'll meet this soldier in Heaven. Because I'd like to talk to him. I'd like to know how he felt that day. I'd like to know how his life changed after that. I'd like to hear the story of how he told his family and friends. I'd like to meet any of them that were changed because of his story of what happened that day. How many people came to know Jesus and the Love he offers through this soldier? Is it possible that he was a part of any of the churches that Paul and the Apostles helped to start? Did this soldier go off and start his own house-church? Is it possible that any of us are his descendants—either through our genetic heritage or our spiritual heritage?

I imagine that as Jesus stood there that day, looking upon those that mocked him in worship, that his heart broke uniquely for each one of them. I imagine that day that Jesus knew every struggle, fear, temptation, and source of guilt for each soldier that knelt there in false-worship. I imagine that Jesus pitied each of them...had compassion for each of them...and yes, forgave each of them.

Jesus marched to that cross willingly. And of course he died for folks like you and me. We're not that terrible, are we? We've not done anything that bad, have we? You know what? We have. Each time we engage in a life of sin, we spit upon Jesus, we kneel in the dirt, and we mock Jesus with our false-worship—indeed, we pound the very nails. Jesus died just as much for those soldiers that day, as he did for you and me. What they did that day, was no worse than what we do when we commit our sins.

I encourage you to kneel sometime today tell God you Love God. And while you're there on your knees, first just spend time in God's presence. Notice how Loving God is. Truly worship. For the word worship simply means to "ascribe worth." And while you're there, confess to God the acts of false-worship you've committed...and ask for healing for the wounds which lead to your sin. But don't get up off your knees before you've asked for forgiveness and received the gift of God's grace—God's Love—for you. Please stay on your knees just a little longer and thank God for the many blessings you have. Start by thanking God for grace. But thank God for so much more. And don't get up off your knees before praying for those who need to know God's Love. Pray for all those other soldiers out there who continue to kneel in false-worship. Pray for everyone around you still living in sin...and especially for those who do not yet know God's Love. And pray that God will use you to reach these people.

I imagine those soldiers kneeling there in the dirt that day in false-worship noticed the profound sadness in Jesus' eyes and the tears that streamed down his face. And I imagine that his tears were just that much more fodder for their taunts. But as you kneel before God today, as you rise, you may see tears there as well. But for you, my friend, they are tears of the greatest joy, for we are told in Scripture that God rejoices over us when we come to God with our Love.

Broken Bootstraps

Psalm 49:1-7, 13-15

I recently inherited a pair of hand-me-down work boots. They were well worn, but had a lot of life in them yet. I grabbed a tin of mink oil and sat on the couch, rubbing the gel-like oil into the leather, reconditioning them and waterproofing them at the same time. It was honestly delightful watching the dry leather become moist and supple once again.

I love a good pair of work boots. The few times in my life when I've truly needed work boots, I have enjoyed them a great deal. There is something very satisfying about sitting on a chair in an old pair of jeans, and pulling your boots on and then lacing them up snugly, ready for the day of physicality before you. You will trod upon mud, and dust, and rocks, and whatever the worksite throws your way, but your work boots will protect you. There is a tremendous sense of the world being right when you're sitting there with a canister of mink oil, rubbing it into the leather of your boots to treat them for the elements. You can see it soaking in and you know that it will protect your feet from becoming wet. It feels good to slip your finger into the loop of your bootstrap and pull your boot onto your foot.

My bootstraps are well worn. I've learned to use them. "Quit your crying or I'll give you something to cry about" was my mantra for many years. I learned to be independent. I learned self-reliance. When the going gets tough, I'm one of the ones who will get going. Because all I really need to know I learned from pulling myself up by my bootstraps enough times.

This is America, the land of the free. Keyword: free. Independent. Not dependent on anyone or anything, or so we're taught. We're taught that life is only what you make of it. In all of these teachings of self-reliance and self-empowerment, it is at least inferred, if not blatantly taught that we are in control of our lives. We have the answers to the questions. We have the solutions to the problems. We are in control of our destinies.

{imagine the sound of a needle being pulled off the record...or for those of you too young to know what this sound is, imagine the sound of your music app telling you it has no wi-fi or Bluetooth connection.}

If you believe that you are in control of your destiny, I have just one question for you: what color are your boots in the world you live in?

Control, in the sense that we perceive to have it, is an illusion. We have moments of control. There are some elements in our lives over which we do exercise some control. But there are simply too many variables at all times existing around us for us to ever truly be in control. It's simply an impossibility. And yet we don't know how to let go of it! This is about the hardest thing for me to do: let go of control. Why? Because I know the answers to the questions and the solutions to the problems.

{BZZZZzzzz...}

"Thank you for playing!" Who will be our next contestant in this game of life? The truth is, I don't know the answers to the questions, nor the solutions to the problems. Because my scope of vision is so very limited. I can only know partial answers to the questions as I perceive them. I can only grasp at simple solutions to problems more complex than I can ever know because of this limit on my vision.

And so I grasp at straws. I grasp at answers. I grasp at solutions. I grasp my bootstraps and I give them a yank and I try to pull myself out of the muck and the mire of my existence and you know what? Sometimes it works. Sometimes, I'm able to pull myself up. In fact, I've done this a lot. But I've looked down at my bootstraps and I've noticed they've become worn. In fact, it looks like they're about to rip through pretty soon. One of these times, I'm going to reach for my bootstraps and I know they're going to come off in my fingers. I will be left standing there with my boots half-on and my bootstraps in my hands and a look of bewilderment on my face. Because then I will truly realize how out of control I really am. With nothing left to pull, I can only grasp at something else.

And in a moment like that, I will truly realize my need for God.

Because God doesn't grasp for bootstraps. God grasps for our very being. God doesn't mess around with that which we have adorned ourselves. God reaches for our souls. God rescues us from the muck and the mire of our existence. God pulls us up, not by our bootstraps, but by our souls and God sets us upon the Rock—God's Love for us.

These boots we've put on can only protect us from some very minor threats. And the straps which we grab to pull ourselves up can only work so many times before tearing off in our hands, leaving us grasping for control and finding none.

The only real, true protection we have can be found in God. In no one, no where, and in nothing else will we find this protection or the answers to the questions, the solutions to the problems, the deliverance from the attacks of evil in this world.

Your boots may protect from some of the small things in life, but they can never protect from the wiles of the enemy we face, nor can your bootstraps save you from the attacks this enemy of ours will throw our way.

Are you still relying on your bootstraps? Are you still carefully rubbing mink oil in them to keep them supple and strong...ready for the time when you'll need them to pull yourself up?

My friends, go get a pair of scissors right now, and lean down with me and join me in cutting off our bootstraps. In doing so, we'll have nothing left to grasp, but the very hand of God...Who will reach down, and "snatch us from the clutch of death." Let's not be those who look out and live for themselves. We know their ending. And we know the ending we're promised in God: a New Life.

Cut off your bootstraps. Surrender control...it's an illusion anyway. But God is no illusion. God is real. God is in control whether you acknowledge it or not. Stop fighting. Instead, surrender...trust in God's Love.

NEW HOPE RISING: PART ZWEI

PSALM 29:9

The surprises we know are coming are the hardest ones for which to wait.

My children didn't believe me.

I read to them the story of the bowling ball, *New Hope Rising*, from my first book, *Untamed Devotions: Stories of a Wild God*. They laughed. They thought it was funny. They laughed even harder at the trouble into which I landed myself as a result. They laughed raucously with loud guffaws and slaps of knees when the bowling shoes sank like a smart phone in a toilet. They snorted, chortled, and tittered with glee when my cousins tattled on me absolving themselves of all guilt like so many penitents petitioning the Pope.

My children did not believe me.

And thus, a couple of weeks later, we were at a garage sale and I saw a gnarled old bowling ball for sale for a buck. Deal. Upon speaking with the proprietor of said sale, I learned it belonged to her now-departed husband Larry, ("May God rest his soul.") who bowled with that very same ball for twenty-seven years on Wednesday nights at the local bowling alley. This ball had a pedigree. It was learned. And it would now pass along a new kind of wisdom.

It was time for a science lesson with the children. I'd show them.

"Kids, would you like to see this bowling ball float?"

"Yeah right, Dad. Like that old thing will float!" they jeered.

"It will," I said with absolute certainty.

"Prove it," they said.

Done. Victory would be mine. I would show the little beasties the error of their ways. I would take them to my classroom and display my wisdom and knowledge for all to witness.

And thus we set out on a Grand Adventure through the back acres out to Coon Creek (pronounced "crick"). I played the part of the Pied Piper, wielding said bowling ball with a line of my offspring in tow.

Down the gentle slope in our backyard, through the gnarled oaks, and then past the remains of an old barbed wire fence we went. Laughter emanated from all as the excitement swelled like a wave about to crest and then crash upon a beach. In the midst of the giggles, a few jabs at dear ol' dad and his crazed ideas, and a slap here and there as mosquitoes enjoined our trek seeking sustenance, or maybe drawing blood to foreshadow the sacrifice the children believed to be imminent.

As we neared the creek, I challenged them to find a part of the creek that was deeper and wider. And after just a minute of walking downstream, we did. Every child wanted to be the one to heave the ball into the swirling flow of the creek. And I wanted to ensure the ball was launched as close to the middle as possible.

I trumped their wishes, and mounted the ball up on my right hand in the mimicked pose of one about to put the shot in a track and field competition. No elaborate spins followed, but rather a deep crouch, and with a twist of my back to the right, hereafter known as "Larry's Lob," I sprang up and to the left thrusting the spherical object of wisdom into glory right into the middle of Coon Creek.

As it arced through the air, all eyes followed its progress in joyful expectancy, children expecting father's failure, and one father expecting vindication.

Thoomp.

Larry's bowling ball entered the swirling flow of Coon Creek, seemingly never to return from its murky depths. I gathered my gaggle and began to walk with the flow of the creek, trying to estimate the progress of the ball I knew was moving with the current and would soon surface.

My dear, sweet children were quite hopeful to show me the error of my ways. And yet, I knew, without any sense of revenge, they would soon be surprised.

The surprises we know are coming are the hardest ones for which to wait.

"There! I think I see something!" shouted my youngest.

"No, that's just a shadow in the water," said his older sister.

The older brother agreed with his younger brother, "Yes, there it is!"

And thus, with much anticipation, Larry's bowling ball began to surface amidst the muddy waters of the Creek.

And like we wait for thunder after seeing the flash of lightning, so we waited that day for the Larry's bowling ball to surface. And that deliciously awful sense of what is coming next, a mixture of anticipation and dread, filled my children as we waited. It's the same feeling as waiting for the thunder, or waiting for the roller coaster to tip over the hill and begin to plummet.

That sense of anticipation is presented so often in what God is doing in the Bible. And truly, it's there every day in our lives. It is with an active sense of waiting, I believe, that we should approach all of what God is doing in our lives.

For when Love shows up, it is like thunder.

To paraphrase Graham Cooke in his lovely British accent: "*When the storms of life hit, do you respond hopelessly by saying 'Oh God.' Or do you look around with eyes wide open saying 'Ok God, what are you going to do next?'*"

I Love that. That deliciously awful sense of waiting for what is coming next. For when God shows up, it is often by surprise, and yet if we are a Hopeful people, we are waiting for the surprise.

The surprises we know are coming are the hardest ones for which to wait.

What surprises are you waiting for, friend? In what areas of your life are you anticipating God showing up? Open your eyes wide. Look. And actively wait. For it is coming.

There's a part three coming to this. Last summer, our neighbor Herb had a bowling ball in his garage sale. I bought it for $1. And our neighbor has a pool.

There just might be a bowling ball showing up in said pool sometime soon. And instead of Larry's Lob, it will be Herb's Heft.

Keep your eyes peeled, my friends. God's surprises are coming.

BREAKING THE RULES

GALATIANS 5:4-6

For much of my life, I have been an ardent rule-follower. If the sign said fifty miles per hour, I would go fifty (notice the past tense). If I was allowed to keep my books from the library for one week, I kept them no longer than one week. Oh yes, for those that know me, this may be hard to believe. But it's true.

It all began when I was a little kid. My parents used to tell me things like, "If you go in the street, you'll get hit by a car and die." And so, I would never play in the street. I believed them. I knew, that if even my shirtsleeve crossed over the boundary of our grass into the cement area of the curb, from out of nowhere, a semi-truck would come hurtling by at the speed of sound and take my arm right off, and with blood pluming forth from my stump, I would stumble around in our front yard and die. My parents would then have to put a white cross there as a memorial to their beloved, child and as a reminder to all children everywhere: "Don't play in the street or you'll get hit by a car and die."

I followed the rules in high school as well. My parents told me horror stories of kids who drank and used drugs who got a hold of some "bad stuff" and died. I believed 'em. I never did drugs, because I knew that I would be the one who would get a hold of something which had a rare, undetectable poison mixed in, and I would consume it and die right there with all the world to see. And people would gather around as I lay there dead with drug paraphernalia on my person and nod knowingly, "We told him so. He should've known better. He got what he deserved."

And this fear of consequences stuck with me for a while. I bought the whole deal. I was a rule follower and incessantly reminded my parents of the rules: "Mo-om (using two syllables and a whiny voice), you're speeding." Or, "Da-ad, the sign says 'No Smoking.'"

When I was a kid, we lived close enough for me to walk to school. On my very first day, my mom walked me down the driveway to say "goodbye" to me as I was to head off to school.

We came to the street and I stopped dead in my tracks. My mother's voice echoed in my head: "If you go in the street, you'll get hit by a car and die." I looked up at the woman I knew as my mother and did a little Socratic reasoning: if I go in the street, I'll get hit by a car. If I get hit by a car, I'll die. My mom is telling me to go into the street where I will surely die. Therefore, my mom is trying to kill me.

My first lesson in the conditionality of rules.

Paul's letter to the church at Galatia, was a reminder to remember the conditionality of rules. It was a reminder to remember the heart and intent behind the rules. It was a reminder to remember God's Love.

In my life, rule-following hasn't made me a better person. It doesn't matter how many rules I've kept. I could keep every rule and still be a pretty rotten person. What matters is the heart. And the guiding force of the heart is Love. And Love is from God, for God is Love.

The churches in Galatia were being overrun by some folks who followed the Jewish law. And they were insisting on returning to the keeping of the codes of the law. In fact, they were judging people at how "good" they were in their faith by how well they kept the law...at how well they followed the rules.

Paul's reminder here is a good one: "Hey folks, it doesn't matter how well you follow the rules. All the rule-followin' in the world ain't gonna make God Love you any more. There is no standard you can possibly attain on your own. The standard has already been attained by One greater than you. And God set the standard for you. God set the standard and met the standard so you wouldn't have to. If you keep the rules, great. If you don't keep to these old rules, fine. Loving God and Loving each other is what matters above any rule. So, if you're keeping our old rules, make sure you're doing so out of Love. If you're not keeping these rules, make sure that you're not just thumbing your nose at the old ways...make sure you're living in Love. Don't let these old "religious" busybodies get in your business and confuse the issue. The issue is Love: God's Love for you, and your Love for God and each other. Got it? Good!"

I'm a first-born in the birth order of our family. We first-borns tend towards perfectionism and over-achievement. We always try to not just meet standards, but beat them. And this letter from Paul to the churches in Galatia is a healthy reminder to us: focus on Love...not earthly standards. Don't just focus on Jesus and how he lived life and what he taught. If we were to do just that, us perfectionists would try to mimic his every action and live his life down to the last letter. We're supposed to focus on the Love-relationship God wants to have with us, and with one another.

If we live in Love, we will strive towards God's standards naturally, because it will flow from being in a living, Loving relationship. However, if we simply focus on standards, without a Love-relationship, we will always find ourselves wanting more and striving to do better.

When we try to meet standards by our own power and might without living in Love, we are in fact, cut off from Love. In effect, we are in exile from God because we trust in only in rules and standards.

It's only when we trust in God, surrendering entirely to Love that we find the standards met, and the Loving embrace of a God who loves us more than any rule. God met the standards because we couldn't do it on our own.

Ask yourself today: "what am I trying to do to please God and why?" Are you trying to be the best Christian you can be by "volunteering" all of your time to your church? Are you giving more than a tithe to gain God's favor? Are you striving to be the best husband or wife or friend that you can be only for recognition? If we do any of these things for these reasons, we miss the point.

When we Love someone, we do these sorts of things naturally. When we Love God, we'll serve at church and in the world as a natural outpouring of our Love. No longer do we "volunteer," we serve out of our Love. When we Love God, we'll give our money to the mission of the church as a natural outpouring of our Love. No longer are we "giving" money to the church, we're deciding what we need to keep to meet our needs. When we Love God, we will be the best husband, wife, or friend we can be as a natural outpouring of our Love. No longer do we try to gain anyone's attention because we know we already have it.

God loves you to pieces whether or not you follow or break any or even all of the rules.

Someone once said: "There is nothing you can do to make God Love you any more. And there's nothing you can do to make God Love you any less."

God Loves you to pieces no matter what.

Are You Dead And Buried?

Colossians 3:3

Some good friends of mine own a cabin up in northern Minnesota. It's a wonderful little place on a river. And over the past couple of years, they've spent a lot of time and money renovating the place to give the cabin a little more ambience. I've been there a couple of times: once B.R. (before renovation) and once A.R. And let me tell you, there is a HUGE difference!

The first time I was there, I noticed little packages of poison all around the place. Now, I'm no Sherlock Holmes, but it wasn't too hard to figure out that their quaint little cabin came with "pets." Great. I was hoping—because I can't tell you how much I'd love to be sleeping and have a furry critter of unknown species dancing on my cranium at 3 a.m. I asked them about the little "care" packages around the cabin and they 'fessed up. Mice.

Over the next couple of years, throughout the entire renovation process, they began to kill off, one-by-one, the beady-eyed little buggers. There was one beast left. And they finally got him...or her...I don't think they checked. Okay, they got it. And it was a little larger than a mouse. It was a cute little chipmunk or a small cuddly squirrel.

Apparently the rodent was a little more intelligent than its miniscule cousins. It must have sensed something not quite right about those cheese-wedge-shaped boxes of poison. It lived for a while in their cabin on the flies it would catch by the windows. But it could hold out no longer. It consumed the last of the flies and finally, with resignation, began to munch the poison.

I imagine the death-throes of the varmint were quite exaggerated. It stood up on its hind legs and grabbed its furry-neck with its little paws, gasping, choking, stumbling about, eyes bulging all the while. And with its last burst of energy, it looked for a quiet place to expire...in between the ceiling of the basement and the floorboards of the main floor.

And there it remained for several weeks.

Have you ever left some leftovers in the fridge for just a little too long? You open the door and an odiferous waft assails your snout. Multiply the rotten leftover smell by ten to the hundred and forty-eighth power and that's what happened when our friends returned to their abode some time A.R.

The little creature was dead and its corpse was decaying. This would be the reason that we bury bodies or cremate them when folks die. Because when we kick the bucket, we stink up the place.

I have two questions for you today:

1. Is your old life dead?

2. Is your old life buried away?

Dying to our old way of life is a tough thing to do. But when you honestly decide to live a life of Love, your old way of life is supposed to be dead. You have been washed clean and made new. But all too often, we forget to bury our old way of life. And pretty soon, things begin to smell a bit rotten.

We have died to our old way of life, but rather than bury ourselves away, we've hidden the corpse of our old way of life in the closet.

And the skeleton in our closet belongs to no-one else but ourselves. We have not hidden away anyone else's remains. We've hidden away our own. And we take them out to dance once in a while. We grasp the bony, decaying hands of our old way of life and dance ourselves into a sinful oblivion, forgetting about the stench we have just unleashed upon ourselves, those around us, and to God.

We're not ready or able to let go. We have not fully surrendered our living in Love. Each time we return to the closet to dance with the remains of our sinful existence, we deny the power of Love to make us clean. We're willful creatures, aren't we? Full of ourselves, full of what we perceive to be life. But as it so often happens, we miss the point. We think we've got a handle on what "real" life is all about and we find ourselves grasping the rotting hand of our sinful existence of which we refuse to let go.

I'm pretty sure I've buried my old way of life many times over. I'm pretty sure I remember standing in the grave, burying away my old way of life. I think I recollect standing upon the pile of fresh dirt that was the reminder of my old way of life. And for a while, I didn't even look back at Old Way Of Life Cemetery. I danced with Joy in New Life.

But then the enemy would masquerade as an angel of the light and deceive me. I would find myself reminiscing about my old way of life. And pretty soon, there I stood, back at Old Way Of Life Cemetery, robbing my own grave. I was not able to leave my old way of life buried. In the crucial moment, I mistook the enemy as an angel of the light, or even willfully denied God, because the truth is, we find comfort in the familiar...even if the familiar is harmful to us. Either way, I deceived myself with my own independence and found myself dancing with the decaying remains of my old way of life.

The only way to keep our old way of life dead and buried is to look only to the Real Life offered to us in God's Love. In every moment, if we turn to Love, our choices will be clear. If we look to ourselves or others, things will become muddied...just like our shoes will become when we return to Old Way Of Life Cemetery.

It's not easy. And I'm pretty sure I will open my closet and find that I've gone back to Old Way Of Life Cemetery because I couldn't leave my old way of life buried. I'm pretty sure I will find myself dancing with the moldering relics of my previous existence again and again.

As long as I'm lookin' to Love, my old way of life stays buried. As soon as I turn away, I'm dancing with my dead self. When I look to God, my New Life gives off a sweet odor to those around me and to God. When I look to myself, and return to my sinful existence, I emit the stench of death and decay.

By the way, my friends extricated the decaying corpse of the critter which had croaked in their ceiling. Things smell much nicer around the place, A.R. But every time they go into their basement and look up at the ceiling, they're reminded of what happens when something dies and is not buried.

WATCH MY STEPS

HEBREWS 3:12-15

My father was a combat veteran. His senses were attuned to sneak attacks and midnight raids. He had reflexes which were lightning quick and sure. And growing up as a child in a house with him made it nearly impossible to sneak something past him.

Keyword here: *nearly.*

I swear that my father went to the basement and loosened floor supports to make certain areas of the hallway creak, thus creating "sound-mines." And so, my sister and I had mapped out the hallway leading from our bedrooms past my parents' bedroom much in the same way my father mapped out minefields when in combat. We knew the exact location of every creaky floorboard. We knew how to turn our door handles from the inside so slowly and quietly that they would make nary a noise. We would then hold the knob on the outside and release it carefully so as not to make any noise upon the exit of our rooms. We knew how to walk down the hall with the stealth of a jungle cat stalking its prey. We tiptoed.

We had calculated, using advanced physics, how to walk down the hall with the least amount of floorboard being trod upon by our sneaking little feet. We were calculating mass distribution and foot-pounds of pressure. We even knew which spots could bear how much pressure before emitting a creak. There were simply some spots we had to step upon, but if we moved quickly, without exerting too much force for too long, the creak would be minimal and most often, the former tunnel rat wouldn't hear.

We had worked out a system of watching out for each other. We would watch each other's feet to make sure that we wouldn't step upon a trouble-spot. We didn't want to set off any sound-mines, blasting forth with a raucous creak, shattering the midnight reverie of our parents' slumber. One of us would take a step, while the other would stand guard, eyeing the other's foot with the precision and care of an Army Special Forces operative. Navy SEALs wouldn't have stood a chance against our covert operations. We even had hand signals worked out to warn the person if their foot were heading towards an impending creak. We would then motion left, right, forward or backwards to let the other know of which way to move their foot to find a safe-spot, free of enemy sound -mines.

We watched our step...and each other's.

We're not so good at that any more...watching each other's steps. We claim that it's "none of our business." In fact, I remember many times as I kid, I would witness some injustice in the world and my parents would flat out tell me, "It's none of our business." I remember one time, I was a young child and we were in the parking lot of a local department store. There was a man who was physically abusing his wife right there in the parking lot and I told my dad to do something and was told: "It's none of our business." I remember that striking a chord of dissonance in my brain. I failed to understand how the well-being and safety of another human being was none of my business. It didn't jibe with me then...and it still doesn't today.

When we watch each other's steps, we are caring for each other. We're caring for personal safety. And we're holding each other accountable.

When you watch someone else's steps and you can see they're headed for danger, you're able to warn them. You're able to let them know they are about to step on a land-mine which will shatter the serenity of their own existence, and probably others around them as well. And when you think about it, don't you want someone doing that for you? Don't you want someone to let you know that you're about to be put in danger?

I think this one's a little easier than the part of watching each other's steps which deals with accountability. Sure, I want you to tell me I'm headed for danger...but I'd rather not have you tellin' me about the things in my life which do not show Love. Being warned about danger and being warned about our moral lapses seem different to us somehow. We're able to accept warnings of danger because we see the obvious care being shown. But it's difficult for us to accept warnings of accountability because we feel that our decisions are "none of their business."

And we're wrong. God tells us here in Hebrews that we are God's business...that as long as this day belongs to God, then so do we. And if we belong to God, then we are God's business and here God tells us to watch each other's steps to make sure that sin doesn't trip us up. We are reminded not to return to the familiarity of our wounds that lead us away from a life of Love.

We are to hold each other accountable. But this is not only hard to receive, it's also hard to give. We live in a society which doesn't take responsibility for its actions. We push our grievances off onto the court system, or to our bosses, or to the police. We medicate and de-sensitize ourselves into oblivion so that we won't have to face up to ourselves or the problems which await us each morning when we arise to face whatever God has in store for us. If we have a complaint against someone, instead of facing them directly and holding them accountable, we're told to take it to our superiors so it can be "dealt with accordingly." If we have moral failings, we hide them in family histories of dysfunction, refusing to accept the responsibility of our own actions. Accountability is both troublesome to give and to receive.

And yet we're called to it out of the care and Love of God who watches out for us. God isn't sneaking around, loosening the floorboards to trip us up with unexpected creaks of temptation to sin. That's the enemy's job. And, quite frankly, we are often our own worst enemies, aren't we? No, God is the one who has trained us to avoid the land-mines which have been placed by the enemy. And part of our training is that we are to watch each other's steps.

And so I tell you today, watch my step...and I'll watch yours. Let's look out for each other. Let's help each other to be care-*full*...and hold each other accountable so that we will avoid stepping on any land-mines of sin which will endanger walking in Love.

Yes, watch your step. Be care-*full* in how you're utilizing your existence. I'll watch my step too. But let's watch each other's steps as well. In doing so, we'll avoid the land-mines placed by the enemy who so desperately tries to distract us from our walk of Love.

TIME TO REBUILD

HAGGAI 1:2-11

Some friends of mine recently bought a new house. Sadly, the house is not yet quite a home. They purchased a house which was, in some ways, in a state of disrepair. I'm sure you've had some similar type of experience at some point. Maybe it was a new used car, or maybe an apartment, or a new house. You moved in, and immediately you created a list of repairs.

Well, in this case, my friends didn't just want to do some minor repairs—we're talking major restructuring. I'm the kind of guy that would prefer to buy the house "as is" and not plan any major projects, other than a coat of paint...or maybe installing a coat rack. My friends are the types that walk in and say, "Oh, that wall's gotta go. And we'll just build a wall here, pour some new concrete over here, and then build a few thousand foot addition over here." Uh huh. That sort of thing boggles my mind. It's kind of like setting the clock in my car.

In many ways, they are rebuilding their home. And a big part of it is happening in the basement. Whomever owned the house before had put in this tile floor. The tile itself was beautiful. The workmanship, however...not so much. If you know anything about tile...anything at all, you know that the tiles must line up with each other, the grout lines must be straight, and it has to be level. In this case, the tiles were off almost an inch in some cases, the grout lines looked more like the San Andreas fault, and the tile itself resembled the tectonic plates underneath the fault—uneven and shifting to the point of almost being on top of one another.

It wasn't pretty. It needed to be torn down and the basement needed to be re-built. And they were just the people to do it. They called us up and asked if we would be available for some grunt-work and I said yes. So, me and three of my boys went over there on a Saturday morning and with jackhammers in hand (no kidding!), we started tearing up tile, ripping down sheetrock, and literally removing walls.

It was *so* cool!

About 2,500 years ago, a similar project was in process. There was a guy named Haggai whom God called to rebuild the temple that had been destroyed by the Babylonians. Haggai was trying to enlist the help of the other Jews in the project. But instead of helping rebuild God's house, they were more interested in rebuilding their houses. Well, as you can imagine, the Almighty wasn't too terribly pleased about it. Didn't God once say something like, "You shall have no other gods before me!" No other gods...not Menard's *or* Home Depot. *None*.

So, like most things that are worth anything, God needed a champion...a prophet...someone to speak God's words to the people of Israel and say, "Hey! Are you more interested in building up stuff for yourself, or for God?" About 600 years later, another prophet (who also happened to be God in the flesh) showed up on the scene and said, "If you find your lives, you will lose them. And if you lose your life for my sake, you will find it." Sounds similar, huh? Those who build up stuff for themselves will lose it...and those who lose their stuff, for God's sake, will find it."

Friends, God will be worshiped. Period. And just a reminder, that worship only menas to "ascribe worth." It will end up that we will recognize God's worth. Whether we choose to do so ahhh...now *that's* what's up for grabs in this whole deal. And God wants to have a place where we can ascribe that worth...where we can Love God.

Why is it that we treat our homes with more respect than our churches? Why is it that when we buy new stuff for our homes, we give our old stuff to the church figuring "it's good enough"? Why is it that the real cathedrals across our fair land are shopping malls and stadiums made from the finest materials, with fountains, beautiful tile, splendor and grandeur while our churches are increasingly warehouses and rented space?

I stand by Haggai today and say friends, "We gotta rebuild the temple!" We gotta rebuild the house of God and worship in it. We gotta rebuild the worship center of our lives and join together in it in the unity of Love. Because if we don't, the very rocks will cry out.

And if we do, I believe we will see the blessings of God's Love poured out to us all.

What "temples" are you building in your life? Where are you investing your time, money, and energy? Are you working to build your house and fill it with more stuff? Or are you working to build God's house and fill it with more people who need Love?

Friends, it's time to do a priority check. I believe that it is time to rebuild.

YOU DE-SERVE IT

MATTHEW 10:34-39

McDonald's tells us that we "deserve a break today." Come on, you know you've earned it. You've slaved all day and night, at work, then at home with your family. You deserve a break, don't you? You've washed the clothes. You've carted kids around the globe to soccer games. You've scoured the sink, washed the dishes, mowed the lawn, washed the windows, changed the oil in the car, and that was all before you left for work! You've even taken time out of your schedule to stop and do something nice for your spouse. Don't you deserve a break today?

There are so many advertisements on TV that tell us that we deserve things. We deserve a fancy car, a new house, a long, tropical vacation, a decadent slice of cheesecake, the finest restaurant reservations, a piece of chocolate, a new wardrobe, that latest music, new shoes, new grooves, a new 84" TV, and a brand new surround-sound DVD player to go with it.

We deserve it...don't we? We're faithful to our employers for years and so we feel we deserve a raise or a promotion. We're faithful to our spouses and we feel we deserve gifts and affection to show their appreciation. We're faithful to our children so we feel we deserve a vacation away from them. We're faithful to our churches so we feel we deserve recognition for what we do. We're faithful to God so we feel we deserve to be shown blessings in a physical way.

We feel we deserve...and we're right: we *de-serve*.

To *de-serve* would be the opposite of serving, wouldn't it?

As soon as we feel we deserve something, we have stopped serving.

And you know what, I'm guilty as charged. There have been so many times when I just feel like I'm givin' and givin' and everyone around me is takin' and takin' and I throw my hands up in the air and tell myself...and God...that I deserve a break! I lay aside my plans and desires for those of my spouse in an effort to serve her, but then I tell myself that I deserve something in return for my sacrifice! I *de-serve* God...I *de-serve* my spouse.

I have stopped serving the moment I feel deserving.

Jesus tells us here to look to God instead of looking after ourselves. As soon as we put ourselves first, we have made everyone else last...including God. No, especially God.

When we feel deserving, we put Love last.

Our plans and our dreams are always secondary to God's. Our wants and desires always take a back-seat to God's wants and desires for more Love in this world. As long as we feel we deserve to follow through with our plans, follow our dreams, fulfill our wants, and satisfy our desires, we are *de-serving* God. Jesus even goes so far as to tell us that if we put our family before Love, then we *de-serve* God. Now that's radical discipleship! God calls for a commitment to Love that is absolute. And really, there can be no absolute commitment without a total surrender. Either we surrender all that we are and all that we have, throwing our hands in the air and crying out "Help, Daddy!" Or, we end up in the same useless, self-serving circle of distrust, disappointment, and disintegration. It's Love first or not. We put Love first or else we *de-serve* God. Period.

And so, as I sit here typing on this cold day, I'm asking myself: *who* am I *de-serving*? And how am I *de-serving* them?

I invite you to do the same with me today. Take an inventory of who or what you are *de-serving*. Are you *de-serving* your spouse? Your children? Your friends? Co-workers? Ministry team?

Are you *de-serving* God?

If we serve God first, we deserve God. If we put ourselves or others first, we *de-serve* God.

WORTH THE KINGDOM

EPHESIANS 6:10-18

You stand on a battlefield. There is a misty haze snaking along the ground in front of you. A barren oak tree stands on the horizon, a reminder of another tree from another time and place...just as barren, but bearing Hope and Promise, nonetheless. Atop a small rise, you see the silhouette of an enemy force. You see the evil commander, muscled and full of spite. There is a glimmer of pride and ruthlessness in his eyes. He sees you standing all alone and figures that he's already won this skirmish. And so he only sends down a couple of his evil minions. The commander practically looks bored.

You examine yourself to make sure you're ready for this battle. You look down at what adorns your body. You see armor of the most brilliant colors. You see a jewel-encrusted sword which should adorn the throne-room of the largest of castles. You see a shield brightly gilded with gold. You stand there proudly. You are assured of a win over such a pitiful force. You look upon them with contempt. They are lower than you. Aren't they? I mean, look at how you are prepared for this battle! Look at your armor compared to theirs! Surely you will prevail. Surely you are mightier than they! Surely you...

Clang! A minion's sword slashes away at you, and you are just barely able to move your shield up to block the attacker. With that one attack, your shield has already sustained a large dent. Your shield will not take much more of this abuse. You regain your composure. You stand tall and take a swing with your bejeweled sword.

And your sword cracks in twain as it is blocked by one of the two minion's swords. And so you retreat up the hill to seek out the wisdom of your Commander.

Once out of range of the evil forces, you stop, turn, and ask aloud to anyone who might be listening: "How can this be? Look at their armor! It's black and plain. There is nothing to it. Is there?" Your armor has been hand crafted to match a person of your station in life. Your shield has been gilded with gold and polished to a mirror-fine sheen. Your sword is worth a kingdom. How can they be beating you?

And you realize in that moment that even these evil minions of your enemy commander have something you do not: they have been equipped and trained by their commander. You have chosen your own apparel. Do you remember as you prepared to leave for battle, your Commander came to you and offered his training and his armor. You rejected it. You said it looked too plain. You turned simple, effective armor down for the armor you had prepared to befit a man of your honor and rank. A proud man like you should have the finest armor, right? A man of your position should have a sword worth a kingdom, right?

And in that moment, you realize your sword is worth a kingdom...but not *the* Kingdom. You realize in that moment, that the shield you bore onto that field was called Spite, your armor was named Pride, and your sword was made only of Greed. The broken sword you still bear falls to the ground with a dull clunk, lifeless jewels now fading into the mist which covers the ground. You leave behind your Greed, and rise up to face your Commander. You hang your head with shame. You realize the folly with which you have acted. And as you plod to the top of the small hill upon which your Commander presides, you begin to remove the armor you have so foolishly donned. Your Pride is leaving you with each piece of brightly enameled armor. And just before you make it to the top of the hill, you take your shield...your Spite...and you sail it into the air...casting it as far from you as possible. A breeze which comes from no-where...and yet...maybe it comes from the hill upon which your Commander stands...catches your shield, scoops up your armor and sword...and carries them as far as east is from west. You see them no more. They are but a faint inkling of memory.

You take the final steps to the top of the hill. Here is your Commander. You look into his face to meet the wrath which must surely be there...instead you see...why, you see only Mercy. How can this be? Look at the foolish-ness with which you've acted! Look at the dead-ended Pride with which you faced the Enemy. Look at the Spite and Greed you used to attack his minions. How can there be mercy? It's almost too much for you to handle. Anger from your Commander, you could handle. But Mercy? It's too much for you and you fall to your knees in front of him. Tears wrack your body. A sob of anguish escapes your lips as your body shakes in grief.

"Rise, my beloved." The words come from your Commander. They are gentle, and yet there is an assured-ness there which catches your attention.

With your head still hanging, you say "But how can you call me your beloved when I have rejected your gifts? How can you speak so gently and look with Mercy upon me when I have scorned You?"

"Because you are my child. You are my dear one. No matter what you do...no matter how far you travel from me...you will always be my beloved. But you have come back to me today! And so I look upon this valley of death from which you have come and I see Hope and Promise instead of the despair and desperation our Enemy wishes you to see. You have returned to me, my dear one, and I welcome you back. Will you now accept that which I choose to offer to you?"

You look up. You see a smile written on the face of your Commander. You see Joy there. You see your Commander in his full glory. And as you look at him, the sun crests over the horizon, and the mist of the morning is blasted away like the shame you felt only moments ago. An elation fills your being as your Commander holds something out to you. It's the simple armor you once turned down. You take it from him. You look at each piece. You didn't see it before, but inscribed upon each piece is a name: your new belt is called Truth, your breastplate Righteousness, your feet are covered in the Readiness which comes from the Gospel of Peace, your shield is named Faith—and you can see that it will extinguish any arrow coming from your Enemy, your helmet is named Salvation, and your sword is the very sword your Commander carries, its name is Spirit—it has written upon it the very words of your Commander!

With a grateful heart and new Hope, you put on the full armor of God which has been given to you. And you stand to face the Enemy yet again. This time, you know the outcome. This time, you know the source of your power. This time, you will overcome, not by your power...but by the very power given unto you by your Commander. There is beauty in the simplicity of your new armor. And this beauty far outshines the over-gilded, outlandishly enameled armor you once carried. The Creator of this armor infuses each piece with beauty, that is its strength which flows from the joyful heart beating within the Creator...your Commander.

The battle will be terrible. The Enemy will stop at nothing to bring you down. This will be no walk-in-the-park, afternoon-stroll battle. This is going to be a life or death war to the finish.

And each time you stand to face the battle, you have a choice: wear the armor you bring to this, or don the armor given to you by your Commander?

As you face the battle of today, what will it be? Which armor will you choose? Your armor may be worth *a* kingdom. But only the full armor of God is worth *the* Kingdom.

WHAT'S IN IT FOR YOU?

MARK 10:41–45

When I was a kid, my mom would make this delectable dish she called Coffee Cake. It's not like any other "coffee cake" I've ever had anywhere else. This stuff is amazing. You take 16-18 frozen bread dough balls, put them in a Bundt cake pan, cover the dough with two boxes of cook-n -serve butterscotch pudding mix, then pour melted brown sugar (approximately 1 cup) and 1 stick of butter, with some cinnamon and vanilla mixed in, over the top, let it rise over night, bake at 350 degrees for about 20-25 minutes and voila! Coffee cake. Grandma Polly's Genuine Coffee Cake.

We would wake to the smell of this tasty treat wafting down the hall, into our bedrooms. Our eyes would snap open like broken window shades. We would then travel at the speed of light down the hall in our pajamas, following the scent of melted caramel. We would look through the door of the lighted oven to see our breakfast baking within. We would paw at the door, whining like hungry dogs. And when it would come out of the oven, we could barely stay in our skin we were so excited. Mom would take a large plate, put it on top of the Bundt cake pan, and then expertly flip it over, not spilling one drop of caramel. She would then take a fork and carefully lift the Bundt cake pan off of the coffee cake.

As soon as she did, the melee would begin. My sister and I would almost become violent at who would get to take a spoon and scrape the pan clean of caramel. We would practically fight to the death over the stuff. It was that good. Inevitably, my mom would have to step in and tell us how ridiculous we were being. She would then make sure there was an equitable distribution of caramel.

As we grew older, my mom solved the problem by baking two coffee cakes...one pan for each of us to scrape. Until that point, my sister and I would fight every time. Not once did either stop and think to ourselves: "Oh I've been first plenty of times. I'll let my darling sibling go first this time." Nuh uh. I thought it was all about me. And she thought life was all about her. And neither of us ever thought of how we could Love, serve, or help the other. In fact, even if she would have asked me nicely, at that time in my life, I would have bargained with her to make sure that I was going to get something in return.

James and John fought about the same kind of a thing. They both wanted to be first in the Kingdom of God. They wanted places of honor. They were asking for this privilege over and above all of the other disciples! They were only looking at what was in it for them.

Let's be honest...*really* honest...when we are asked to do something, how often do we think to ourselves as we're being asked: "What's in it for me?" I know I'm guilty of this big time. If I'm asked to do a favor, I often think to myself: "Woohoo! Now I've got a favor coming back to me!" Mentally, I pull out my little tally sheet and put a little hash mark in the "You've Got One Comin'" column for whomever the poor soul is who is now in debt to me, unbeknownst to them.

And that's one of the kickers right there: so often people are in debt to us and they don't even realize it! They've requested our assistance only to find that our intentions were none too altruistic and they must now endure a life of indentured servitude. Do we really mean it when we ask someone: "How may I help you?" Do we *really* care about them? Does our heart truly break for them in the same way God's does?

We should not be emphasizing membership in our churches in the way we have in the past. Membership, for too long, has implied perks. Finish this statement: "Membership has its _____." In fact, at many churches, you get a discount on certain "services" if you are a member! Weddings and funerals for members cost less or are even free. However, for non-members...for people who may even know God's Love, we charge them an arm and a leg—and potentially their very souls, because our concept of privileged membership has gotten in the way of them being able to see the true difference it makes in your life to know God's Love.

Hello! Why are we doing this? Why are we building un -scalable walls around God's Love? Who do we think we are being God's gatekeepers? Heaven is not a gated community! No more! We must break these chains of insanity which we are using to bind those not yet knowing the Love of God. Membership is not about privileges...it is about responsibilities. It's not about us...it's about God.

We're even asking what's in it for us when we evange- lize! We look for glory and recognition. "Hey! I led four people to Jesus last week." We try to get people to come to our churches, not because we want them to grow in a life of discipleship, but because we want to reap the benefits of their discipleship to make ours a little easier.

Jesus said he came to serve, not to be served. And Paul, in his letter to the church in Ephesus reminds us that we're not supposed to Love folks thinkin' that there's somethin' in it for us. We're supposed to Love them like God does: unconditionally. God tells us that there's nothing we can do that will make God Love us any more or any less. We're supposed to Love like that!

So, what's the answer?

It's called Servant Evangelism...lookin' at the people around you and always asking the question: "How may I help you?" without asking for anything in return, at the same time, letting people know why we are serving them.

At one church we had a free car wash open to the public. We had about 15 to 20 cars come through. Most people, I'm sure, assumed that we didn't really mean free when we said "Free Car Wash." I would guess that most folks thought that we were accepting donations. Out of the cars that did stop, there were several who tried to offer us money in exchange for our services. When we replied "We appreciate the offer, but we're not doing this for a financial donation. We're doing this because we want you to know that God Loves you." People couldn't believe it. In fact, one guy tried for a while to argue us into accepting his cash donation. So enculturated was he in our system of payment for services rendered that he had great difficulty in accepting the gift. We didn't see any of those people come back through our doors. But that's okay. Because that's not the point. The point is for people to be served and to know that God Loves them.

All around us, there are opportunities to serve. Every day, you wake up with a day filled with such opportunities. Help is wanted...*needed*, in fact. And we have the power to help...because God came to help us first.

Over what coffee cakes are you fighting? In which things are you seeking to be first, over and above everyone else, disregarding their needs? My dear friends, the Love of God is far sweeter than any coffee cake. And if something like coffee cake causes us to fight because it tastes so good, is it any wonder that the Love of God, of which

James and John had only a foretaste, could cause such a fight?

The Love of God is not something to be fought over, but something to be shared. And we are never to ask what's in it for us...because we already know: the very same Love that's in it for everyone...a Love so great God sent Jesus to take our place in the sacrifice.

Stop asking "what's in it for me?" Rather, when you see someone, ask gracefully, "what would you like to be in it for you?" And then surprise them by giving it to them.

P.S. Many ask about Grandma Polly's Coffee Cake recipe, so that's why I included it in the beginning. But no fighting over it...okay? Maybe you'd better go buy an extra Bundt cake pan right now!

WHAT LIES BENEATH

ROMANS 1:18-23

It was Christmas time, and the small shop owner was fretting over whether or not this would be a good year for sales. Last year was wonderful, but things hadn't been as good this year. And the shop owner was finding that things were getting a bit tight for him. What could he do to make it so that sales would be good? What novelty could he provide? What angle could he use? His was a small gift shop. The kind at which you find knick-knacks, cards, baubles, and figurines. How could he attract attention to his small shop in the midst of the glitz of the malls at this time of the year? What could his little shop offer that they could not?

Standing behind his humble cash register, he scanned the shelves of his shop. Upon them, he saw each little item, carefully dusted, ready to be purchased. But nothing stood out. As he stood there thinking, he couldn't figure out how he could ever compete.

The bell over his door rang. A customer! He tried not to hawk over the person. But was still curious nonetheless.

After a couple of minutes, he approached the woman, who was standing there holding a small porcelain figurine in her hand. "May I help you, ma'am?" the shop owner asked.

"Actually, I was just looking." the woman replied. But then she stopped and cocked her head to one side as she examined the figurine. "You know, if this were only gold or silver, I would buy it. But it's just plain old white porcelain. I have been searching everywhere for something like this in gold or silver and have only found these in white porcelain."

"Really?" the shop owner asked. "I'm sorry. I've never seen these in silver or gold."

"That's too bad," the woman said. "I've heard of so many people looking for just such a thing."

And as the poor little shop owner stood there, the idea came to him: he could take these figurines and paint them with gold and silver paint. He would be the only shop to offer such an item.

"Uh...ma'am. What if I told you that I could order these in silver or gold? Would you be interested then?"

"Heck, yeah!" she said excitedly. "How long will it take for you to get these in?"

"I can have them by tomorrow," he replied.

"Great. I'll take two of these in silver and two in gold." And with that, she wrote down her name and number, left them with the shop owner, and exited the store.

The shop owner promptly closed his store, went to a local hardware store, and purchased a good supply of gold and silver paint. He stayed up all night painting his entire stock of white porcelain figurines with the gold and silver paint. And then stocked his shelves full of them. He then spent time creating a sign to put in his shop window with a picture of a gold figurine painted on it. He went to bed, getting only a few hours of sleep, before it was time to reopen his store the next morning.

The woman came back, just as she had said, and purchased her four figurines. The shop owner was greatly pleased. In fact, he was able to jack up the price on the figurines by more than five dollars each. And the woman didn't even bat an eye at the price. She was willing to pay it. She was also greatly pleased.

"These will be perfect decorations in my house! I'm going to tell all of my friends that you have these!" And with her gratitude duly expressed, she left.

The shop owner was overjoyed. Maybe, just maybe, he could make something out of this Christmas.

As the day went on, several more customers came in, looked at the gold and silver figurines, and expressed their delight. He soon realized he would have to order more and get some more paint.

He did. He made up hundreds of the figurines and by the time Christmas came, he sold out of them. He had even doubled, and then tripled the price because the demand was so high.

He had made Christmas into something more than it was going to be. He figured out a way to make his profit.

Christmas came and went. Only a few days after the blessed holiday, the original woman came back. She did not look pleased anymore. She was carrying the bag in which he had sold her the figurines. She marched up to the counter, and took them out and laid them out before the shop owner.

She was so angry, that her bottom lip was quivering with her rage. A tear was forming in the corner of her eye.

"You deceived me." she finally said.

"Beg your pardon, ma'am?" the puzzled shop owner asked.

"You had better beg more than that," she replied. "I want my money back. These are only the cheap white porcelain figurines I saw that first day. All you did was paint over them. I know your secret. The truth is out and I'm going to tell everyone. You are a liar and a cheat."

The shop owner apologized profusely, gave the money back, and sat there dejectedly looking at the figurines before him. He picked one up, and noticed that the paint was beginning to flake off of it. You could clearly see the white porcelain underneath.

He had covered up the truth of what they were. And the customers couldn't see the truth because they wanted so badly to have the gold and silver figurines they thought they were getting. They were blind to the truth. If they really would have stopped to look, they would have seen. But their desire was too great. And the shop owner capitalized on their blindness. And now, the truth was out in the open for everyone to see. He was a fraud. And he had hoodwinked his customers, substituting cheap figurines, with a facade of gold for the real thing.

Every day, God offers us the real thing, but so often we trade it for the cheaply painted figurines we'd rather see. We have gotten so used to lying and wrongdoing, that it doesn't even phase us to substitute a false image for the real thing. We'd rather not live up to the standards of what God offers, and so we create idols that will meet up to our standards. We trade God's standards for ours, and end up holding onto cheaply-painted, dead-end, empty-promise idols.

Nothing that God offers is cheap. God provides Love instead of the dead-ends we so often choose. And God offers a promise full of Hope and meaning.

How come we so often settle for the lies of cheap figurines when God offers us the Truth of a romance with God?

Because it's easier. We don't have to do much of anything to satisfy these cheap figurines. We don't have to live differently. We don't have to surrender anything but a couple of bucks. We can continue on living meaningless, sin-filled lives.

But God, the Real-Thing, has higher standards than that. God is Truth. And Truth will accept no cheaply-painted substitutes. For no matter how gilded they are, the lie is still there.

What can these lies give you that the Truth that is in Love can not? Nothing that is worth anything, to be sure.

Into what lies have you bought? What cheaply-painted figurines adorn your spiritual houses? Trade them in—no, better yet, *smash* them on the floor and ask for God to wipe the slate clean today.

Sadly, there are many churches and pastors in this world that offer the same cheaply painted figurines of cheap grace. They tell only half of the Gospel. They only tell the part about God Loving you. They only tell about the Grace. But they leave out the part about having to radically Love everyone around us.

God offers you a promise through Love, that is better than any figurine...better than gold itself. God offers you Truth and Meaning, direction in this aimless world, Hope in the midst of chaos and death. A life of direction and forgiveness is offered to you so that you can radically live in this same Love. This is a promise better than silver and gold.

As you clutch your cheap figurines, hiding their lies under facades of gold and silver, remember that God holds the very world in his hands, and you along with it. Drop your figurines, open your arms to God, surrender to God's embrace, and find the Truth of God's Love waiting there for you.

And God Winked

Luke 2: 8-12

There's a light breeze, blowing the tall grass, making whisper noises which foreshadow the song which will be sung later this very same night. The crickets are chirping, adding their harmony to the whisper-song of the grass.

There is a group of shepherds there, reclining in the grass, keepin' an eye on their flock of sheep. Some of them slept, getting some sleep before it came their turn to take shift on the night watch. They probably had a few small campfires going to further scare away predators and to warm up some food. As they camped there, some of them probably wondered about the bright star in the sky. I'll bet some of them even gossiped about it, coming up with possibilities for its purpose. This is a scene, just itchin' to be painted. It's a Kodak moment.

The world in solemn stillness lay. It is a silent night. The midnight is clear. Bethlehem is lying still. All is calm.

For the moment, that is. Little do those poor shepherds know what's coming next.

Sheepherders are prepared for predators. They know that at some point in their illustrious careers tending flocks of sheep, they will have to do hand-to-paw combat with some nasty fang-bearing critter which would love to have a midnight snack, munching a sheep or two. Sheepherders are prepared for bad weather. They know they'll have to find shelter for themselves and quite possibly weather some bad storms. They're prepared for long times away from family and friends. They're prepared for travel. They're prepared to search for a lost sheep.

But the shepherds we read about in this story were nowhere near prepared for what would break the silent reverie of their midnight clear.

Half-dozing sheepherders, leaning upon their staffs, as the wind whispers through the tall grass are shocked from their peace by an angel which just appears out of nowhere.

I imagine some of them going into attack mode, thinking of protecting their sheep, almost attacking God's messenger. I imagine that some of them were too bewildered to do much of anything, standing there with mouths agape. And I imagine that some of them were so startled that they soiled themselves from the sudden shock of the angel's appearance.

Can you blame them? They didn't have much experience with angels. When they were going to shepherd school, there was no elective course in *Angel Appearances and What To Do About Them*. The story tells us that they were terrified. I imagine that when the shepherds who went into attack mode or were bewildered truly realized who had just appeared...an angel of the Lord!...that they all became terrified.

I imagine this rough, gnarled group of guys huddling together in fear, knees trembling, some of them begging for mercy, others crying. Have you ever been afraid like this? Have you ever truly been terrified? Because these men were. They were truly terrified. Fear was gnawing away at the edges of their sanity, reducing them to a group of knee-knocking, simpering children.

The first words out of the angel's mouth? "Don't be afraid."

Some of them probably thought, "Uh huh. Yeah, right! Don't be afraid? Easy for you to say Mr. Bright-and-shiny-Angel-of-the-Lord-guy. You just pop in out of nowhere and we're supposed to 'not be afraid.' Excuse me while I go clean out my shorts."

But others of them, I'm sure, were able to hear the tone of the angel's voice. They were able to hear the peace there. They were able to hear the words of God through the chaos of this event. These shepherds breathed a sigh of relief. And as their brains began to give way to peace instead of fear, a new thought dawned upon them: "Why on God's green earth are you coming to us? We're just a bunch of stinky ol' shepherds out watching our flocks by night. How come you're not visiting that ol' King Herod? Why aren't you going to the priests in the temples? What do you want from us?"

The angel chuckles lightly, adding a note of Joy to this chaotic moment. "What do I want from you? I don't want anything *from* you. That's not why I came. I want something *for* you. I want to tell you some news."

"News? God sends an angel to us to tell some news? We don't get it." responds one of the more experienced shepherds.

"It's precisely because you are who you are that God has sent me to you. God's kinda gettin' tired of being so predictable. So, this time around, God's going to mess with things a bit. Instead of sending angels to the people you'd expect, God has sent me to a young virgin and her fiancé, a group of foreign scholars, and you guys! The kings and priests of your world need some shakin' up. So, here I am, talkin' to you...shakin' things up."

The shepherds could appreciate that. They understood the joke. And they suddenly had a whole new appreciation for God. A new joy filled them...although it could also be called humor. And with smiles beginning to appear on their faces as each one of them in turn began to realize how God was upending their social order, one of them asked, "So, what news do you have for us?"

"Are you ready for this?" asked the angel, "You've known for a long time that God was going to send a Messiah, right?"

"Yup." responded the shepherds.

"Well, get this...God's sent the Messiah, all right, but..." the angel had to stop to laugh. He finally got control of himself, took a deep breath, and said, "but the Messiah is a baby!" with that, the angel burst into tears, he began to laugh so hard.

The shepherds didn't quite get it at first. And so one of them asked, "Well, He's like some sort of a king or something, right?"

"Well, yeah. Technically he's a king. But this king has just been born in some motel-stable down there in Bethlehem. And his throne is a smelly old feeding box used for the stable animals. You see guys, God's not interested in all of the religious trappings...God is tired of all the pomp and circumstance you've added to worshiping God. That's why God's sent me to regular folks...unexpected folks. That's why God has sent the Messiah as a helpless baby who will grow up with common people. God wants to be known by the Least, the Last, and the Lost, because the most, the first, and the found already know God and have missed the point."

"What's the point?" asked a shepherd.

"The point is this: Love God...Love each other. But you know what...I shouldn't say anymore. I'll let your new Messiah tell you...when he learns how to talk!"

The shepherds all laughed at that.

"Now, just one more thing," said the angel.

"Sure, what's that?" asked the sheepherders.

"God would like you guys to head down to Bethlehem and go see the baby. He'll be in that stable I was telling you about."

"You got it. We'll go and see him. Anything we need to bring?" they asked.

"Nope...well, nothing material anyway...just bring your sense of humor...and bring your hearts," said the angel.

And so the unlikely heralds of the Messiah went to see him. They laughed and talked along the way. They wondered about the future. They wondered how things would change. They wondered how this Messiah would save them. And they laughed some more at the thought of the Lord of the Universe having such a great sense of humor.

And when they got there, Joy exploded from them as they saw the Messiah lying there in that feeding box. The poor virgin and her husband looked tired, but a great sense of peace filled them.

And here is how I imagine the scene to have happened...that as the smelly sheepherders approached, the Baby Messiah King looked at them...*God* looked at them...and winked.

And the sheepherders smiled. And then they knelt to worship...to Love.

Unlikely Heralds

Matthew 2:12
Luke 2:20

So the wise men and the shepherds all took off. They'd followed stars and listened to choirs of angels. There must have been a lot on their minds as they traveled. The wise men traveled a long distance. With how many people did they have a chance to share the Good News that the Messiah had come? Were lives changed as they traveled? Are there people who have relationships with Jesus today who are spiritual descendants of those with whom the wise men shared the Good News? Do you know of the Messiah because of the wise men? Could be.

How long were the wise men gone? Were they kings in their own lands? Some texts say kings...some say wise men. Whatever the case, we know they were followers of astrology. They searched the heavens for signs of what was to happen. They looked for portents in the stars to tell them the future. And God spoke to them in a language they could understand. God put a bright star in the sky so they would understand that something great was happening. God used the stars to signal to them that a great king had been born upon the earth. God spoke in their language. God chose them to be messengers.

The shepherds went back to their sheep. They traveled back to their homes and along the way, they praised God. It says that they "let loose." That means they weren't being quiet about what they'd seen. It means they were ardent in their proclamation of the birth of the Savior!

They were untamed in their faith. And their words were probably crude and as un-poetic as you can get, like their crude exteriors, used to tending sheep. Their words were possibly laced with the profanity of the day: "Holy sheep dung! We just came from a freakin' stable and saw the Messiah!" God went directly to the shepherds with an angel. God met them where they were. God chose them to be messengers.

I love that the first evangelists were foreigners and smelly shepherds! Isn't that great? God chooses unlikely people to be messengers of Love. Do you know what that means for you and me?

We are the very kinds of people God would choose to be messengers. You and me...we're unlikely people. Think of where you've been. Think of the things you've done. You and me, we're not rulers. We're not even mayors, let alone presidents or kings. You and me, we're just ordinary folks with great hang-ups, fumbling faults, and more than likely, colorful pasts that we'd have to explain if we were to ever run for any of these offices. If Jesus were to be born today, I imagine that God would choose a biker gang and some Buddhist priests from Nepal to be messengers. God would choose the homeless man you saw downtown. God would send people like the Hispanic busboy who cleared your dishes from your table the last time you ate out. God would send the prostitute hanging out on the street corner who thinks she's got good news, but whose life will change forever once the angel talks to her. That Viet Nam veteran you saw in his raggedy old army jacket, Johnson was his name...you know, the guy with the scraggly beard, missing his left arm who flinches every time there's a loud noise...He's God's messenger of Love.

You and me, we're not any better, nor are we all that different. We stink just as badly as those shepherds and we're foreigners in a strange land, trying to find a language so we can all understand each other.

God chooses unlikely people to herald what God is doing.

You and me? Hah! God chose *us*? Hello! What is God thinkin'? Why us?

Well, it's precisely because we are who we are that God came to us and spoke to us in our own language and met us where we were. God spoke to the wise men in their language and met the shepherds where they were. God did the same for us. With all of our hang-ups, faults, and the screw-ups of past and present, God came to us, speaking in a language we could understand and our lives have been forever changed. We are the very wise men and shepherds of this world.

Are you laughing yet? Me too.

But think of it...God chose you and me! Boggles the mind, huh? Why us? It's pretty simple, it's because we have faults...it's because we've screwed up...it's because we can speak the language and have "been there, done that, and bought the T-shirt" that God has come to us. We can understand and relate. We've been down in the dumps. We've been trod upon at one time or another by the cultural elite of this world. We've been taxed and taunted, exploited and excluded. We know what it is to be alone. We know hurt. We know betrayal. We understand what it's like to want more and receive less because at one time or another, we've been a stinky shepherd. We understand what it's like to be a foreigner because at one time or another, we've all experienced not being allowed to "join in any reindeer games."

"For unto us this day is born a Savior, who is Christ the Lord." That's very poetic, ain't it? How will we say this in a language that the weary and downtrodden, the homeless and the mortgage-bearer with the 8.5% variable interest rate can understand? What words will we use? How will we "let loose?" Will our words be poetic drivel, cheesy and beige? Or will we speak with the colorful slang languages we each use in our own lives?

And so we find ourselves on our way back to our homes and villages, called to let loose in the very same way those shepherds and wise men did. We find ourselves, with all of our hang-ups, faults, and colorful pasts being the very messengers of God!

We are unlikely heralds, huh? What's God thinkin' anyway?

DIGNITY REDEFINED

MATTHEW 1:18-19

In 1994, I began serving my first church. It was a United Methodist Church in Arlington Heights, Illinois. I was young, inexperienced, and very excited...especially as we drew nearer and nearer to Christmas. I will never forget my first Christmas as a pastor and planning for the Christmas Eve worship service. You know the deal. Candlelight. Angels. Reading the Christmas story. And of course, singing *Silent Night*, raising your candles high, singing the sweet refrain, "*Slee—eep in hea—ven—ly peace.*" Sigh.

Now, what was causing me a bit of consternation was the fact that a local group home of developmentally disabled adults attended the church. And they were there most of the time. And for the most part, they were very well behaved. Except for when it came to singing. They sang at the top of their lungs, and not particularly in tune. And most of the time, it was sweet. They didn't know any better. They didn't know that they should sing quietly, blending in with those around them so they wouldn't stick out. They were presenting a problem to me in my Christmas Eve planning. How could we possibly sing Silent Night in reverence and awe with the members of the group home yelling out the words? You see, I didn't want my Silent Night to be blemished by their awkward behavior. I didn't want to sacrifice my dignity, nor the dignity of the occasion.

And yet, what I failed to realize, is that my thoughts of their behavior, had already cost me my dignity altogether.

For truly, what is more dignified: to be concerned with what all those around you are thinking and how you're behaving and whether or not everyone is in tune as you sing Franz Gruber's famous Christmas hymn? OR, to lose yourself completely in Love, singing to God at the top of your lungs?

Dignity redefined.

Here is a Christmas story over which we gloss each year when it comes time to read about the silent, holy night in that little town of Bethlehem where the world in solemn stillness lay: a teenage girl on the verge of being stoned to death. Silent night, holy night, huh? Mary, a young woman betrothed to Joseph was found to be pregnant...and Joseph knew he wasn't the father. And for her perceived actions, the punishment was clear: death by stoning. This is a death difficult to imagine any time, let alone in the midst of traversing malls to buy the perfect gifts for our loved ones. It is a death difficult to imagine, let alone in which to partake. Put down the wrapping paper for a moment and try to imagine instead bending down to pick up a fist-sized stone and then hefting it at a young pregnant woman.

A young woman, just barely past girlhood, her dignity shattered, as she thought of what her family and her husband-to-be would think of her. And yet, the angel was clear, wasn't he? "You will be with child and give birth to a son, and you are to give him the name Jesus." Luke 1:31 So, a virgin is suddenly with child...and it's not the child of her betrothed. This was not her plan. It certainly wasn't Joseph's. To anyone else, the young maiden was a disgrace, a shameful wretch, an undignified out-of-wedlock mother. But to the God of Creation, she was the mother of the incarnate God. The mother of Love.

Dignity redefined.

Is the story of young Mary fore-shadowing of a later woman in a similar situation? She's caught in adultery and is drug into the town square, publicly derided for her sin. And as the angry mob stirs deeper into the oblivion of their self-righteous fervor, a rabbi steps into their midst. Did Jesus bend down to write in the dirt so as to avert his eyes in an effort to preserve this woman's dignity because the memory of his mother in the same situation was overlaid upon that moment? Jesus preserved her dignity, just as his earthly father Joseph had preserved Mary's.

And as you read this, my friend, what undignified actions of yours come to mind? Over what have you sinned? Have you held hatred in your heart? Have you clung to bitterness, rather than seek to forgive? Have you lusted after that which you have no justification for, and yet have sought with all your heart in a futile attempt to assuage the pain you've endured? Let's cut to the chase now. Friend, as you draw nigh to Christmas, to celebrate Jesus' birth, what sins are yet before you?

Will you come to the manger this Christmas with them? Instead of laying gifts of gold, frankincense, and myrrh before Jesus, won't you kneel before him and lay your sins at his feet? Because truly, the greatest gift you can give, is to set aside your own dignity, humbling yourself, seeking Grace.

When you seek out Jesus, in humility and Love, He honors his Word by "remembering your sin no more." The God of this universe, more powerful than presidents, kings, and even capitalism chooses to preserve your dignity. Your sins are cast into the depths of the deepest sea. They are as far as the east is from the west. They are blotted out by his bruises. For the preserver of our dignity—this Jesus—was "bruised for our iniquities... pierced for our transgressions," sacrificing his dignity to preserve yours—and at the same time redefining the word.

Pre-serve. Hmmmm...now there's a thought. Jesus died to pre-serve you. He was serving you before you were even born. He was *pre*-serving you. And his pre-service has *preserved* you for all eternity to be at his side.

Because here's the thing, my friend, Jesus came to redefine *your* dignity by sacrificing *his*.

When the *Silent Night* moment rolls around for you this Christmas, remember the song of the developmentally disabled group home members. Without a care in the world for what anyone around them thought, they burst forth in a song so beautiful, and so pure, that it didn't need a certain melody because it was filled with such a dignity of undeniable, overwhelming faith—sung at the top of their longs, with no particular tune.

> *Silent night. Holy night.*
> *All is calm. All is bright.*
> *Round yon virgin, mother and child.*
> *Holy infant so tender and mild.*
> *Sleep in heavenly peace.*
> *Sleep in heavenly peace.*

Dignity redefined for you and for me.
Merry Christmas, dear friend.

LOOKING FOR CHRISTMAS

MATTHEW 2: 1-2

Each year I go in search of Christmas. I look for it. I get into the whole active waiting thing of Advent. I look for stories in social media that speak of Christmas miracles, and self-less acts of giving, and...and...

And I'm often left with this empty feeling as I realize the best evidence for original sin is waiting ten minutes for a parking place at the local mall the day before Christmas because there is some gift I've put off until the last minute. And just as the car finishes backing out and I prepare to pull in, some depraved soul whips in just ahead of me, all but crushing my Christmas spirit.

This year has been no different. And I've been looking. Hard.

I've scoured my social media feeds to no avail. I've awaited a magical starlit moment viewing Christmas lights. Nope. In fact, as I've come upon the anniversary of my mom's death that occurs just before Christmas, I've found myself quite lacking in Christmas spirit, looking for something and not finding it.

But one thing I forget is that *Christmas often finds me when I'm not looking.*

As we walked into the hospital room of my then-wife's ex-husband, Christmas found me. And it wasn't gentle this time. It was not a *Silent Night, Holy Night* moment. More like a healthy dose of perspective...God putting me in a headlock and giving me a healthy dose of Divine Noogies.

You see, so often Christmas shows up for me as a warm-fuzzy feeling replete with goose-bumps. But this time was different. For this man for whom I should probably have had some sort of hard feelings, instead caused my heart to grow three sizes that day.

Christmas often finds me when I'm not looking.

As I was driving there, I was meeting my wife to pick up my stepdaughter from her weekend with her dad and grandparents. He was in the hospital because his MS had progressed and would be transitioning into assisted living. As I drove, I thought it would be nice to stop and pick up some coffee and a treat for my wife and step-daughter. And as I pulled into to purchase it, I felt compelled to purchase coffee and a treat for him as well.

Nope. No warm-fuzzies. No tears of sappiness. No *Silent Night*. Just something...Some*one* prodding my heart to purchase treats for my wife's ex-husband. Raising my eyebrows with a mild, surprised irritation, I obeyed.

"Fine," I thought. "I'll buy the stupid coffee and donut for this...this..."

"This Child of God, whom God loves very much...and who has done nothing but speak highly of me to his daughter, giving her permission to Love me."

{deep sigh} "Seriously, God?" I thought.

I parked at the hospital and made the trek to his hospital room. As fortune would have it, I arrived before my wife and stepdaughter. I was going to wait in the lobby for them to arrive so we could go up together.

"Go up and say hi," said my Inner Voice.

"Oh, you have got to be kidding." I responded aloud. Yes, aloud. In the hospital. Several visitors and medical staff turned and looked at me. I smiled sheepishly and pushed the call button for the elevator. Seriously, coffee and donuts are one thing...but go up and visit him? Come on!

And as I made the trek up those several floors, and walked down his hallway to enter his room, I felt something stirring within my heart. I knocked on the door to his room. "Come in!" he said.

For just a second, I hesitated, questioning the Voice. Turn and go to the lobby! He has no idea who just knocked. "Go in." I heard in my heart.

I took a deep breath, and I did.

And I was greeted by Christmas. I'd been looking. And it wasn't where I thought it would be. Not by a long shot. It was in the hospital room of my wife's ex-husband.

"Merry Christmas, Shane!" said Matthew.

"Merry Christmas to you, Matt." I said, with grateful humility. Because truly, I knew this was God's doing. I couldn't have put this together. No...I *wouldn't* have put this together. But God would...and did.

Christmas often finds me when I'm not looking.

Just like God.

God often finds me when I'm not looking. Because so very often, I'm looking where I shouldn't be, or where I want to, or where it feels good to look, but not where God wants me to. And so the challenge is this: to be both vigilant and aware, looking for what God is doing, and showing up for it on the occasions when you do find it, but to also be vigilant and actively on the lookout for when God shows up and surprises you...and to be ready to obey one of Jesus' most challenging commands: "Follow Me."

And so I sat here, reflecting on my budding friendship with my wife's ex-husband, and I had to chuckle. God certainly has a sense of humor.

And once again...I've found Christmas...or rather, Christmas found me.

And I shall do my best to follow.

It's Not About What You Want

Tonight I was going to meet one of my buddies for a bite to eat, and then we were going to go to a church he used to attend many years ago. I knew my buddy had a rough week, so I tried to surprise him with a few things I knew under normal circumstances he'd appreciate.

But not tonight. Tonight he was irritable and criticized my attempts. I was flabbergasted and frustrated. I wanted to do something nice for him. I wanted to make him smile. I wanted to bring joy to his Christmas. I wanted...

I wanted.

I never bothered to ask what *he* needed.

Sometimes Christmas isn't about what we want, but about what others need.

While I wanted to do nice things for my friend, he needed something else. Yes, my intentions were good. My heart was in the right place. But I wasn't listening to his heart.

And shouldn't it be? Shouldn't it be that what we want is exactly that...what others *need*?

Sometimes Christmas isn't about what we want, but about what others need.

Christmas is about exactly that. It's about Love coming into the world to transform hearts so that what we want is to fulfill other's needs...to Love one another.

Each year I look for Christmas. And it always surprises me. And this year it didn't surprise me in any of the things I wanted...but in exactly what I needed...to see and hear the needs of those around me.

As I held my candle high singing the final refrains of "*sleep in heavenly peace*," Christmas came to me...at exactly midnight...Christmas morning.

Sometimes Christmas isn't about what we want, but about what others need.

So what is it that you need this Christmas? Please let me know if I can help. Because I will do my best. And that's exactly what I want for Christmas.

Merry Christmas to you, my dear friend.

HOW I RUINED CHRISTMAS...AGAIN

I'll never forget the Christmas Eve service of 2005. We had spent weeks going over the passages of Scripture we'd read that night. We crafted the song selection to go with the flow of the evening to highlight experiences and create a Christmas Eve into which everyone could enter. We had tradition. We had innovation.

All was calm. All was bright. Candles were lit. Emotions were high. It was a beautiful service in every way.

We had three services that night. And all of them turned out wonderfully. Our Scripture reader was a delightful woman with a slight drawl. And for the life of her, when it came time to read the passage about Quirinius being governor of Syria, she just could not get it right.

In the first service, Qui-RAY-nius was Governor of Syria. And the second, it was Qui-RYN-ius. And in the third, and no, I'm not even kidding, Queer-anus was Governor of Syria. My pastor friend and I were shaking, we were laughing so hard.

And this was not what ruined Christmas.

We chose mostly very traditional songs to be shared Christmas Eve: *Hark the Herald Angels Sing, God Rest Ye Merry Gentlemen, O Come All Ye Faithful, Silent Night,* and *Away In A Manger.*

And that was how I ruined Christmas. For you see, I'd penned a refrain to *Away In A Manger.* Yes, all of the verses were exactly the same. But I added a refrain. And a sweet, perfectly lovely older woman I'd never seen before at church came up to me afterwards with tears streaming down her face, wagging a finger at me to let me know that

I'd ruined her Christmas. I added the following refrain to her song, and I'd gone and done it. I ruined Christmas.

A manger a feeding box holding our King
God sent a baby salvation to bring.
The star that night shone forth like the day
On Little Lord Jesus, to show us the Way.

It seems innocuous enough, doesn't it? And truly, it was, as it was penned with the best of intentions.

Ah, but *often our expectations get in the way of innovation.*

For you see, that night, a sweet, wonderful older woman came to participate in her Christmas traditions. She came to hear the same old songs. She came to sing *Silent Night*...to hold her candle aloft. And she came as well to hear *Away In A Manger*...as it had been sung since she was a little girl. A song that granted her comfort, as she sang to Jesus asking for him to be near to her...to be close by her forever and Love her.

She did not come to hear a new refrain penned by some upstart pastor, even though the passage he penned spoke of the very same Little Lord Jesus...and the Star...and...

And her expectations got in the way of innovation.

I went and did it again this year. I ruined Christmas.

As I sat in the oncologist's office just a couple of weeks prior to Christmas with my son, Tucker, and the woman who would become my wife, Dani, on speaker phone, we heard him say these words: "The cancer is back, and it is not beatable."

Oof. There it was. A punch to the gut. I was prepared to hear the cancer was back. I was prepared to fight, and to do chemotherapy, and radiation, and have more surgeries. But I was not prepared to hear that the Beast had returned, and that it would eventually take my life.

We all wept. Including my oncologist. It was a difficult day, at best. That night, through tears and with a wry grin and a little laughter, my future wife said to me: "You know, you really suck at giving gifts!"

I ruined Christmas.

But just when we think something has been ruined, we find that Love shows up and what we perceive to be ruined, has actually been saved.

For it is true, isn't it, that *often our expectations get in the way of innovation.* Our sense of what should be gets in the way of Love showing up and doing a new thing. We expected to have a lovely, Currier and Ives, Norman Rockwell sort of a Christmas with eggnog, lights, trees, presents, carols, etc. But the new thing we received was a renewed sense of Hope...of the value of Life...the value of each day...the value of Love...of LIVING Life as we'd often discussed before the cancer came back IN ALL CAPS.

In the midst of the shock of wondering how many Christmases we would share together, our hearts exploded with Love. We became more urgent. We decided together then and there that we wanted to LIVE all of our days together with an urgency to Love and to Serve those around us...and each other. We decided that we would fight this Beast with all we have. We decided that we would Love each other through it all. And we decided to do something we weren't going to do for at least five years: get married.

Our expectations almost got in the way of innovation. And what we thought had been ruined, had actually been saved.

This Christmas, evaluate your expectations...and keep your eyes peeled for Innovation. Jesus is always there showing up when we least expect it, and most need it, doing a new thing...not to mess with our expectations, but to "ruin" Christmas in such a way that it is actually saved.

May you have a *Ruined* and *very* Merry Christmas!

EPILOGUE: SHE JUST STOPPED LIVING

JOHN 10:10

His voice was like gravel, coated with 10w-40 oil, all rough and smooth at the same time. He sat next to me on our shuttle from the Denver airport to the hotel. He appeared to be in his mid-fifties. There was a joy for life in him, with a hint of loss tugging at his smile. He seemed both happy to be alive in each moment, and yet a wistfulness did not allow it to come into its fullness.

I stuck out my hand, "Hi, my name is Shane. Are you coming or going?"

He turned his head to the side, with his tousled fading red hair, much like my own. A slight smile split his coppery beard. "My name's Dale. Coming home."

"And what brought you to the Midwest, Dale?" I asked.

"My son plays football for Macalester. I try to make it to as many of his games as I can."

"That's really cool, Dale. I'll bet your son appreciates it."

"Yeah, in fact, I'm considering moving to the Twin Cities."

As he was boarding the shuttle, I was just reading a piece by Elizabeth Gilbert on the idea of Freedom in one's life...choosing to live Free, rather than forcing one's self into others' depictions of what it means to be "good." To be good...acceptable...to fit in...toe the line...not stand out...to assimilate. To be beige.

And so, with a profound sense of kismet in the moment, I grinned like the madman of Walden Pond and said, "You should, Life is too short."

The flinch, barely perceptible, startled me. It was obvious I'd blundered into some old wound. His head dropped forward just a bit, and he smiled wistfully and repeated my words back to me, "Life *is* too short. My wife died five years ago at the age of 47."

"I'm 47." I said.

That realization hung in the moment for both of us. For me, echoes of Thoreau bounced wildly about my noggin like popcorn seeds in a hot kettle. For him, memories of his bride.

"What was her name?" I asked.

"Elaine. She was an ICU nurse," he said.

"Elaine," I repeated. "My wife is a nurse. How did she die?"

"Nobody knows. They couldn't determine a cause. She just stopped living."

She just stopped living.

Let that sink in. Read it again.

She just stopped living.

As autumn leaves die and fall to the ground as I pen this, I am forced to the question: "How have I stopped living?" It's a tough question to face, isn't it? We must get real and honest and vulnerable with ourselves to answer. Because then we begin to discern the areas of our lives where we have fallen into a rut, have settled, or worse, never truly lived at all.

The promise of God isn't for an OK life...a beige life...a so-so, meh, whatever life—it's for an *abundant* life! Life to the full...to the max...turned up to 11...LIFE in ALL CAPS! And there is so much evidence for this. Look at the vibrant colors, rich smells, delicious tastes, fantastic

More Untamed Devotions

sounds, and oh-so-wonderful feeling touches available all around us! The world is extravagantly ALIVE. And we do our best to walk around glued to our screens, necks craned at ungodly downward angles, scrolling away with our thumbs to see the latest statuses posted in the effort to portray a full life.

Let's stop portraying a full life...and start LIVING one. I realize that the cover of the journal in which I am writing this has the Latin words Carpe Diem on it. Seize the day. LIVE!

She just stopped living.

My friend, have *you*?

POSTSCRIPT

I just found out that my friend Joe took his life this week.

A couple of months ago, Joe reached out to me asking if we could have a cup of coffee together. We hadn't talked in several years. I agreed to meet him.

Joe confessed to me that he had been battling marijuana addiction for many years unbeknownst to his family. But recently Joe was unmasked. His employer required a random drug test and he asked his son to urinate for him in the cup. Shortly thereafter his wife found one of his pot pipes in his truck. He chose to blame it on their college-aged daughter.

Joe was unmasked. And Joe decided to start LIVING.

Joe decided to get clean. And he began to confess his struggles to his family and friends and to go to meetings for his addiction. I invited him to church and he came! And a couple of weeks later, he brought his wife. The healing had begun.

246 | Shane Allen Burton

I don't know what happened. I don't know what broke down for Joe. But I know he decided to stop living. Something inside him was hurting so badly...and he masked it well...that he made the choice to don his mask, and end his pain.

Friend, if there is anything I want you to hear from me it's this: you don't have to wear your mask with me. Whether we sit together in a church pew or on a barstool, I will offer you a hand of friendship, a listening ear, and the Love of God.

Post Post Script:

I'm ending this book with the knowledge that this cancer is back and will more than likely take my life much sooner than intended. But one thing I can be sure of: that for whatever time I have left, it will be spent LIVING life in ALL CAPS, doing my best to Love those around me extravagantly. And so I say it again: I'm here for you. Take off your masks. Be real. I've got a shoulder to lean on or cry on. I'll cheer you on or just listen...or even give you a little spiritual ass-kicking if need be. But I'm here.

And I'm ALIVE...doing my best to #LIVEINALLCAPS!
And I Love you. *Yes, you.*

Untamed,

Shane Allen Burton

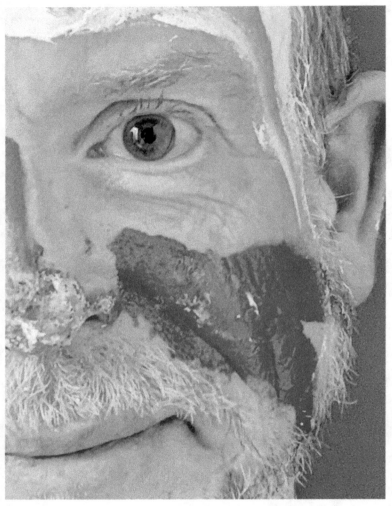

Author photo by Danielle Palmer

About the Author

Shane has been a pastor in both established churches and church plants throughout his many years of ministry. For much of that time, he was a pastor in the United Methodist Church, including one church plant, but also led a Baptist congregation, a non-denominational church plant, a Lutheran church, and has also been a worship leader in multiple congregations.

He has worked as a pastor, insurance agent, pawn broker, mortgage professional, executive director of a publishing company, supervisor in an oil refinery, editor, as well as retail management and consultant work. He currently resides in Hudson, Wisconsin with his beautiful wife Dani, and between the two of them have 9 children: Patrick, Josh, Rachel, Tucker, Cole, Isaac, Darby, Lilliana, and Zander.

Shane loves good coffee, good whiskey, fine chocolate (any chocolate for that matter), reading books, Grand Adventures with his wife Dani, writing, editing, musical performance and composition. His child-like Untamed faith is contagious and he will challenge you to LIVE your life in ALL CAPS!

Shane has been battling Stage 4 Esophageal Cancer since February of 2018 and continues the fight. He says to never give up Hope, for Hope is a dangerous thing.

You can reach him at:

Shane Allen Burton
shane@shaneallenburton.com

CPSIA information can be obtained
at www.ICGtesting.com
Printed in the USA
FSHW010250030720
71390FS

9 781595 987679